Appetizers

Appetizers

SOUPS, SPREADS, SALADS, HORS D'OEUVRE, PASTAS AND MUCH MORE

BONNIE STERN

Random House
Toronto

Published in 1990 in Canada by Random House of Canada Limited, Toronto

 This book is printed on acid-free paper.

Canadian Cataloguing in Publication Data

Stern, Bonnie
  Appetizers

ISBN 0-394-22150-8

1. Appetizers. I. Title.

TX740.S74 1990   641.8'12   C90-094328-9

DESIGN: Brant Cowie / ArtPlus Limited
FRONT COVER PHOTOGRAPH: Copyright © Robert Wigington
BACK COVER AUTHOR PHOTOGRAPH: Skip Dean
FOOD STYLIST: Olga Truchan
ILLUSTRATIONS: Wayne Terry
EDITORIAL: Shelley Tanaka
PAGE MAKE-UP: Heather Brunton / ArtPlus Limited
TYPE OUTPUT: TypeLine Express Limited

Printed and bound in Canada by John Deyell Company

To my sister, Jane —
remember that like appetizers,
good things come in small packages.

Acknowledgments

SPECIAL THANKS ALWAYS goes to my dedicated and hard-working staff at the cooking school and shop — Maureen Lollar, Susan Bate Santos, Lettie Lastima, Julie Lewis, Sadie Darby, Linda Stephen and Robert Butler.

Thanks and love also go to my number one taster, my husband, Ray, and the rest of my support group at home — Daphne Smith, Tina Lastima, my parents, Ruth and Max Stern, and Fara Rupert.

And special love goes to Mark and Anna, who still don't eat anything I cook (except for pancakes). But I love them so much anyway, and I'll keep trying.

Appreciation goes to Brant Cowie, Robert Wigington, Olga Truchan and Wayne Terry for turning food into art in their own ways.

I also want to thank my editor, Shelley Tanaka, for editing my work just the right amount — letting me sound like me, but a bit better; and Doug Pepper, Ed Carson and the crew at Random House.

Contents

Introduction

THE FIRST THING that people taste when they come to your home is the appetizer. And that's why I think it is so important that it be very special. It doesn't have to be fancy or take a long time to prepare, but it should be something that you are proud to serve and that really makes guests long for more. Appetizers should "tease the appetite" — work as a temptation of the delicious things that will follow.

I think there are three basic components of good cooking. First, you have to be organized and think things through carefully. Second, you have to have some basic knowledge of how to cook and follow recipes (and know when not to follow them, too). And finally, you have to cook with love and enthusiasm. I can help you with the first two points, but the third and perhaps the most important has a lot to do with your own feelings in the kitchen. So don't forget your sense of humor, don't be afraid, and try to cook only for those you love and care about. After all, the love you put in your food is the secret ingredient that even the finest restaurant doesn't have access to.

Bonnie Stern
TORONTO

1

Techniques

Today there are as many wonderful ways to start a meal as there are different ways to entertain. The chapters on spreads and hors d'oeuvre offer things you can serve as a little nibble before dinner with a glass of wine, to say a friendly hello and welcome. Many of them can also be served in a more formal way as a sit-down first course and, of course, they are also perfect for cocktail parties. The chapters on first courses, soups, pastas and salads include recipes ideal for a sit-down dinner, but many of them also make great luncheon or light supper dishes. Also, don't forget that many people, both at home and in restaurants, like to make a meal of a few appetizers, rather than have an official main course. Add that's fine, too.

In this chapter I have given you tips and suggestions to help you with the recipes in this book and cooking and entertaining in general. And throughout the book there is additional material about ingredients and techniques. Check the index to find information about individual subjects.

Menu Planning

Menu planning can be confusing to both professional and home cooks. But there are certain guidelines and, if you follow them, your menus should be well composed.

The main thing to remember is that ingredients and flavors should not be repeated. For example, if you serve smoked salmon as an appetizer, don't serve salmon steaks for the main course. Likewise, a smoked salmon appetizer that contains dill should not be followed by another dish with dill.

However, if an ingredient doesn't dominate, it can be repeated. If you serve a pasta with a tomato sauce as an appetizer, for instance, you may not want to serve a tomato salad, but a green salad containing some tomatoes shouldn't be a problem.

Think about color, texture and shape. Obviously, you wouldn't serve a meal in which everything was brown or white, but a menu that has been designed with a lot of color in mind may not need to be garnished. (Vegetables of different colors also often contain different vitamins.) If one dish is crunchy, accompany it with things that are softer. If one sauce is silky, another should be chunky. If you are serving a variety of appetizers, think about their shapes and imagine how they will look together on a platter. (Look at the cover photograph of this book to see how shapes can work for you.)

Think about the temperatures of foods. Foods served cold and at room temperature not only add variety, they can also be made ahead and do not need last-minute heating. (When you are having a big cocktail party, heating things up can become a problem. Always think these things through ahead of time!)

Don't feel that everything you serve must be expensive. You don't want to show off to the point where your guests feel like the poor relatives from the sticks.

If some dishes are rich and heavy, serve others that are low-fat and light. Give guests choices, and if you are planning a multi-course feast or a great variety of appetizers, be sure to serve very small portions. You want people to feel well fed, but they should be able to walk away from the table when the meal is over!

Plain and fancy, easy and difficult and fast versus time-consuming are other things to keep in mind. Even though it is fun to serve exotic dishes, you would be surprised at how many people still enjoy simple foods. And if every dish is complicated and time-consuming to make, not only may you hate entertaining by the time your guests finally arrive, you'll end up with too many culinary "stars" of the show.

Although everyone likes to cook the things they themselves like the most, when you are entertaining, the food preferences of your guests should come first. Of course, you should like the food, too, but those crazy new recipes you got in California may not be perfect for your great-aunt and uncle (or they may be perfect — only you know). If you do not know the people you are inviting, cook things that are generally familiar and well liked.

Party Time

Although I love to entertain, there have been many times when I have wondered, "how did I get myself into this mess, anyway!" And I know that many people feel the same way. I once had a party for seventy-five people and really cooked my heart out. After all, could I really call a caterer and show my face again? As everyone was eating merrily, I overheard comments like, "of course it's good. *She* made it." But, in fact, no one actually told me they loved everything. I was so depressed and thought I'd never have another party. Then one of the musicians, whom I had never really met, came up to me and said, "I don't know who catered this party, lady, but the food is the best I've ever had at one of these things." He made my day!

Feelings aside, when you are entertaining, the best way to keep yourself calm is to be organized. Make lists, and then make lists of your lists. (And don't forget to read them!) When I organize a dinner party, I write down when to serve what, when something should go into the oven, come out of the oven, etc. If you do this, you will have far fewer things to worry about, and you won't find the salad in the refrigerator when you make breakfast the next morning!

When you are planning how many hors d'oeuvre to serve, think about what else people will be eating, what time of day the party is, where people have come from and where they are going. If people are coming to dinner and you are serving hors d'oeuvre as a first course, serve four to six "pieces" per person.

For a dinner party for eight people, I would probably prepare no more than two or three different recipes. But if no appetizer is to be served at the table before the main course, I would increase the "piece" per person to six or seven, and the selection to three or four different items.

For an evening cocktail party, I would count on people eating about twelve to fifteen hors d'oeuvre each, and I would probably make about six to eight different kinds. If you are having people over after work, and they will then be going on to dinner, serve six to seven hors d'oeuvre per person and about three or four different kinds. If you serve many different items, there will be too many competing tastes, and guests won't be able to really appreciate all your efforts.

If you are entertaining a small group and there are enough end tables and coffee tables, you can serve appetizers that require a fork. But at a cocktail party, you can't expect people to balance a wine glass, a plate and a fork, and still eat and be happy! Serve only finger food.

Sometimes it is convenient to have dips and pâtés on side tables or on the bar, but if you have a lot of people in a small space, they often cannot move around enough to serve themselves easily. Only you can judge whether the space you have can accommodate your guests comfortably, but if I have more than twelve people, I like to pass foods rather than have them in one place. Or you could do a little of each.

If I am entertaining more than twelve guests, I like to hire a waitress to help me. That way I can enjoy my party, too. If someone tells you she entertained a hundred guests and she did the barbecuing and her husband was the bartender and everything was great, it's only because the person has never had proper help! Once again, if you can afford it, having help just lessens the chaos. If you have a good waitress and bartender (a bartender often helps the waitress and does much more than serve drinks), when the guests have left, your home should scarcely look like you had a party!

I don't like to serve appetizers piled up on large trays. Instead, I use smaller platters and have second sets in the kitchen that I can whip out when the first platter begins to thin. That way the food always looks fresh and not picked over. I also like to space out the food, so that guests can pick up something they want without destroying three other items on the platter.

And don't forget to think about the logistics of your house. I usually have the bar and the food in separate (almost opposite) rooms, so that people keep moving and avoid traffic jams.

Garnishing

There are all kinds of ways to make food look beautiful without spending a lot of time on garnishes. If you plan your menu with color in mind *(see page 1)*, often the food doesn't need much garnishing at all. You can also serve your food on unusual platters. I have a large collection of serving pieces and decide which ones to use by looking at the food. If the food has a lot of color on its own, I'll use a solid-colored or white platter with an unusual shape, but if the food is rather plain, I'll dress it up by serving it on a more colorful dish.

Table cloths and napkins can also help dress up the food. Centerpieces can be made from fruits and vegetables as well as flowers. Bread in different shapes can garnish the table, and lettuce, greens and herbs of all kinds can be used to dress up platters and food. If you need a large platter and don't have anything that will do, cover a baking sheet with foil and line it with doilies or greens.

If you are serving fried foods and want them to stay crisp, don't serve them on a bed of greens. The moisture from the greens will cause the food to wilt almost immediately.

Here are some ideas for more structured garnishes. Always be on the lookout for new ideas. If you go to a restaurant and see an unusual garnish, don't be afraid to ask how it's done. Sometimes the chef will say no, but most professionals love to share ideas.

TOMATO ROSES: Use a firm red tomato for this classic garnish, and if you haven't done it before, buy more than one tomato! With a small, sharp knife (I like to use a serrated one), cut the base from the tomato but leave it attached. Then start peeling the tomato in one continuous strip about 1 inch (2.5 cm) wide. Break off the strip about halfway around the tomato. Curl the strip around its base, then finish peeling the tomato in a slightly narrower strip. Curl that tightly and insert it into the center of the large piece. (Every tomato rose you make will be slightly different.)

You can make cherry tomato roses in a similar manner. Buy large, firm cherry tomatoes, but peel them in one continuous strip. You can also pat the tomato strips dry and spread cream cheese on the cut side. When you roll the peel up, you will have a two-tone tomato rose.

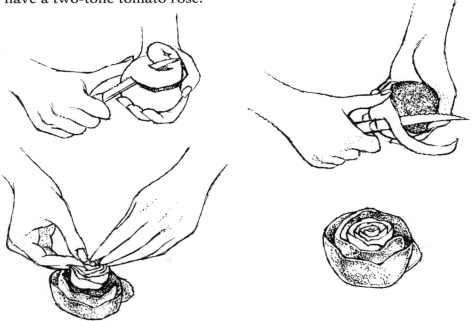

SMOKED SALMON OR HAM ROSES: Cut strips of smoked salmon or ham about 1 1/2 inches (4 cm) wide. Curl them up to form roses. For tomato roses, I work from the outside in, but for smoked salmon roses I usually start with a tight center and then drape more strips around the outside.

CUCUMBER FLOWERS: To make cucumber flower containers to hold individual portions of dip or sauce, use English cucumbers, as they are usually narrower and longer than regular cucumbers, have fewer seeds and unwaxed skins. Cut off the point so the flower will have a base on which to stand. About 2 inches (5 cm) from the base, cut into the cucumber as shown, curving the knife slightly to the inside middle area. Do this in three or four places around the cucumber. Break the section off, then scoop out the seeds with a melon baller. Pat the inside dry and fill. Continue with the rest of the cucumber. You should get five or six tulip-like flowers from each cucumber.

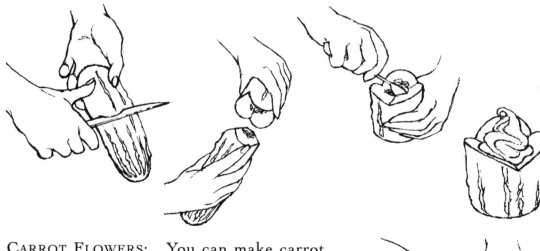

CARROT FLOWERS: You can make carrot tulips like the cucumbers above. They look great in stir-fries, and they make cute little cups for scooping up dip on a vegetable platter. You can also make carrot "daisies" by cutting V-shaped slits lengthwise around the circumference of the carrot. When you slice the carrot, the slices will look like flowers.

LEMON TWISTS: Lemon twists are a lovely garnish for fish dishes or anything that has a lemony flavor. If you like, you can "strip" the lemon first using a stripper so that the slices are fluted. Then cut the lemon into slices about 1/4 inch (5 mm) thick (or thinner). Cut each slice from the center to the outside edge, then turn one of the cut edges one way and the other edge the other way.

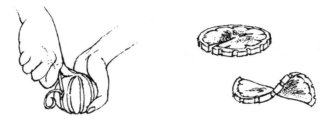

LEMON OR TOMATO CUPS: These pretty little cups can be used to contain dips or sauces. Although you can buy a special V-shaped knife to make this garnish, you do not really need one. First cut a small piece off both ends of the lemon so the cups will stand upright. Draw a fine line around the circumference of the lemon. Then, with a narrow knife, make V-shaped incisions all around the lemon, cutting through to the middle. Gently pull the two halves apart. Remove the pulp with a grapefruit knife or spoon, and pat the inside dry before filling.

SAUCE DESIGNS: These can be used on platters, soups and desserts. Place the sauce in a squeeze bottle, piping tube with a fine nozzle, or in a Ziploc-type bag (seal it and cut off a tiny tip, as shown). Use contrasting colors and be sure (especially in the case of a soup) that the mixture you are garnishing is heavier than the garnish! Easy things to pipe are sour cream, crème fraîche and lightly beaten whipped cream.

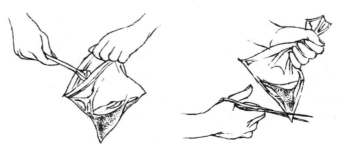

SPIDER WEB: This looks so fancy and expensive at restaurants, it's hard to believe it's so easy. Place some sauce or soup on a flat plate or in a bowl. Pipe concentric circles of contrasting sauce or sour cream over this sauce. Pull a chopstick, toothpick, or point of a knife through the sauce toward the center at 12 o'clock, 3 o'clock, 6 o'clock and 9 o'clock. Then, at 1:30; 4:30; 8:30 and 10:30, pull the knife from the center to the outside edge.

AVANT GARDE PATTERN: Make concentric circles as you would for the spider web, but simply pull the knife through the circles in a whimsical way, swishing this way and that.

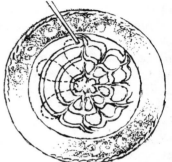

SOUTHWESTERN PATTERN: If you are making a Southwestern soup or appetizer, pipe Zuni patterns on top. Once, Olga Truchan, a food stylist I often work with, made the most amazing design on a red pepper soup by reproducing a pattern she found on a pair of silver earrings in a Southwestern store!

Freezing

I have never been much of a "freezer" person. I usually cook things fresh, and so even if I have things in the freezer, I often forget they are there until it's too late. Someone once told me to make a list of what I had, but then I forgot to look at the list! So much for bad habits.

However, I have to admit that if you do make things ahead and freeze them, last-minute guests can be entertained royally. And, if you are having a party, you can freeze things in advance to leave yourself a lot less to do at the last minute. Do keep stock of what you have in the freezer, though, and tape the list to the freezer door. And keep it up to date.

Nothing really tastes better after having been in the freezer, nor does it get better the longer you keep it there. Just about everything you freeze will keep for three to six months, but you should use things up as quickly as possible.

Generally it is better to freeze things uncooked rather than cooked. Freezing things uncooked gives them a chance to recover from any "freezer" taste they may have acquired.

Most things that have pastry or a pastry wrapper should be baked from the frozen state. Just add about one-quarter the cooking time for small items. Larger items may require twice the cooking time.

When you are freezing something, clear out a shelf in your freezer first and be sure your freezer is set at the lowest temperature. If you are freezing individual items like phyllo triangles (they freeze very well, by the way), line a baking sheet with plastic wrap, arrange the triangles side by side in a single layer, and freeze them for a few hours or until frozen. Then pack them into airtight freezer bags or plastic containers. That way they will not stick together, and you can defrost as many as you need at a time. When it comes time to bake them, arrange them, frozen, on a baking sheet in a single layer and bake them from the frozen state, adding one-quarter of the cooking time (i.e., 25 minutes instead of 20).

Certain things freeze better than others. Anything wrapped in pastry (phyllo triangles) or made of pastry (ricotta twists), anything with cream cheese or anything rich will usually freeze very well. Raw fruits and vegetables (unless they are going to be pureed and/or cooked) do not freeze well at all. And cooked vegetable mixtures (like spicy eggplant) get a bit watery after they are defrosted, but this can sometimes be remedied by recooking them.

Remember not to refreeze anything unless it has been cooked. For example, if you buy raw frozen shrimp, you shouldn't refreeze them after they have thawed, unless they have been cooked.

The longer you want to freeze something, the better it should be wrapped. Freezer burn and freezer taste are quite common to foods that have been frozen for too long or foods that are not wrapped properly. I used to wrap things for the freezer in everything I had — plastic wrap, foil, freezer paper and bags or plastic containers. Now I usually just use airtight freezer bags or plastic containers. Squeeze as much air out of plastic bags as possible to help prevent freezer burn; the bags will also take up less room! And be sure to label all food clearly, including quantity and date.

A Lighter Side

Everyone is trying to watch their weight and limit their fat intake these days. To this end, I have added some notes at the end of many of the recipes on how to reduce calories and fat. Some recipes, such as Oriental Eggplant Spread and Spa Pizza, are already low in calories and fat. And some recipes just wouldn't be the same in taste or would need too much adjustment in a lighter version. In this case, I often feel it is better to make it the right way and then cut calories by eating half as much.

2

Spreads and Dips

Tapenade

This flavorful mixture has recently become very popular with the renewed interest in the cooking of southern France. Serve it with crackers, toast, French stick, or as a dip with vegetables. For a different taste but more spreadable consistency (that is fabulous for sandwiches), use 4 oz (125 g) cream cheese instead of the olive oil.

Makes 2 cups (500 mL)

1	7-oz (184 g) tin flaked white tuna	1
6	anchovies, minced	6
3	cloves garlic, minced	3
1/2 cup	black olives (preferably Kalamata), pitted and finely chopped	125 mL

2 tbsp	capers, finely chopped	25 mL
2 tbsp	red wine vinegar or lemon juice	25 mL
1/2 tsp	freshly ground black pepper	2 mL
1/2 cup	extra-virgin olive oil	125 mL
3 tbsp	chopped fresh parsley	50 mL

1. In food processor, blender or with a mortar and pestle, combine tuna with anchovies, garlic, olives, capers, vinegar and pepper.
2. Beat in olive oil slowly and steadily. The mixture should be the consistency of thick mayonnaise. Taste and adjust seasonings if necessary.
3. Place tapenade in an attractive bowl and sprinkle with parsley.

A Lighter Side: Instead of using olive oil, add low-fat unflavored yogurt to the tuna mixture. It will taste very different but it will still be delicious.

Salmon Rillettes

This is one of my very favorite recipes. I brought it home from my most recent trip to France. My adventurous friend, Mary Risley, who owns a cooking school in San Francisco, arranged a do-it-yourself barge trip along the Saône River. We cooked, we cleaned, we ate, and we laughed a lot as we steered our way through the locks. Serve this with lightly toasted brioche, French bread or black bread.

Makes approximately 2 1/2 cups (625 mL)

1 1/2 lb	fresh salmon fillets	750 g	1 tsp	Dijon mustard	5 mL
8 oz	smoked salmon	250 g	1/4 cup	extra-virgin olive oil	50 mL
1/4 cup	chopped fresh chives or green onions	50 mL	1/4 cup	unsalted butter, softened	50 mL
2 tbsp	chopped fresh tarragon (or 1/2 tsp/2 mL dried)	25 mL	1/4 cup	crème fraîche *(page 11)* or sour cream	50 mL
2	egg yolks	2	1/2 tsp	salt	2 mL
2 tbsp	lemon juice	25 mL	1/4 tsp	freshly ground black pepper	1 mL

1. Fill large deep skillet with water and bring to a boil. Add fresh salmon fillets and cook for 7 minutes. Turn off heat and allow salmon to cool in the liquid. Salmon should be slightly undercooked in the center.
2. Chop smoked salmon and combine with chives and tarragon in large bowl. Reserve.
3. In food processor or blender, blend egg yolks with lemon juice and mustard. Add olive oil in a thin stream. Blend in butter and crème fraîche. Add salt and pepper. Mixture should be smooth and creamy, somewhat like a mayonnaise.
4. Drain cooked salmon well. Break flesh into large flakes, removing bones and skin. Combine with smoked salmon and herbs.
5. Gently combine "mayonnaise" with salmon. Taste and add more salt, pepper or herbs if necessary.
6. Line a 9 x 5-inch (2 L) loaf pan with plastic wrap. Spoon mixture into pan. Cover well and refrigerate for a few hours. Unmold and slice into serving pieces. (Mixture may break apart slightly.) Garnish with herbs and smoked salmon roses *(page 5)*. Or you can serve this from a terrine or serving dish. Pack mixture into dish, cover and refrigerate for at least 1 hour. This can be served cold, but it is easier to spread if it has been out of the refrigerator for 20 minutes before serving.

A Lighter Side: Omit egg yolks. Use 1/2 cup (125 mL) low-fat unflavored yogurt instead of olive oil, butter and crème fraîche.

Hummus with Sesame

This is a great last-minute appetizer. I always have the ingredients on hand, and it only takes a few minutes to prepare. What's best, everyone always seems to love it. This version tastes very similar to traditional hummus bi tahina, but it has fewer calories. Serve it with sesame crackers, pita chips *(page 18)*, vegetable slices, black bread or tortilla chips.

Makes approximately 1 1/2 cups (375 mL)

1	19-oz (540 mL) tin chickpeas, drained	1
2	cloves garlic, minced	2
3 tbsp	lemon juice	50 mL
3 tbsp	extra-virgin olive oil	50 mL

1/2 tsp	Tabasco sauce	2 mL
1/2 tsp	oriental sesame oil	2 mL
1/2 tsp	ground cumin	2 mL
2 tbsp	chopped fresh coriander	25 mL
	Lemon slices	

1. Place chickpeas in food processor fitted with metal blade. Puree coarsely. (If you are using a blender, add 1/4 cup/ 50 mL water and puree in two batches.)
2. Add garlic, lemon juice, olive oil, Tabasco, sesame oil and cumin. Puree until the mixture is as smooth as you wish.

3. Transfer mixture to serving bowl, sprinkle with coriander and decorate with lemon slices.

A Lighter Side: Omit the olive oil and use 3 tbsp (50 mL) water to thin mixture.

CRÈME FRAICHE   *In Europe, crème fraîche is a high-fat (sometimes up to 48 percent fat compared to our whipping cream at 32 to 35 percent fat), thick, rich cream that is used on desserts and in cooking. Because its fat content is so high, it does not break down when used in sauces, and it adds a wonderful flavor — not quite as sweet as whipping cream but not as sour as sour cream.*

You can buy crème fraîche, but it is quite expensive, so here are two homemade versions:

Combine 2 cups (500 mL) whipping cream with 2 tbsp (25 mL) buttermilk. Cover and allow to rest at room temperature for 18 to 24 hours, until thickened. Refrigerate for a day or two before using. It will keep for about 3 weeks.

Or, combine 2 cups (500 mL) whipping cream with 1 cup (250 mL) sour cream and continue as above.

You can also whip crème fraîche, although you may have to thin it with a little whipping cream first if it is too thick.

Walnut Bread with Sesame Seeds

This bread is easy to make and tastes great with the Gorgonzola Pâté *(page 21)* or just about any spread! Be sure the walnuts are very fresh. If you do not have a French bread pan, simply knead in more flour (to make the dough firmer and prevent spreading) and bake on baking sheets.

Makes 2 loaves

1 tbsp	granulated sugar	15 mL	1 tsp	salt	5 mL
1 1/4 cups	warm water	300 mL	2 tbsp	walnut oil or vegetable oil	25 mL
1	envelope dry yeast (1 tbsp/15 mL)	1	1 cup	coarsely chopped walnuts, toasted	250 mL
1 1/2 cups	whole wheat flour	375 mL	1	egg white, lightly beaten	1
1 cup	all-purpose flour (approx.)	250 mL	1 cup	sesame seeds	250 mL

1. Dissolve sugar in 1/4 cup (50 mL) warm water in a medium-sized bowl. Sprinkle with yeast and allow to rest for 10 minutes, or until yeast bubbles up and doubles in volume.
2. Meanwhile, in a large bowl, stir flours and salt together and reserve.
3. In a separate bowl, stir 1 cup (250 mL) warm water with walnut oil and reserve.
4. When yeast has risen, stir down and combine with water/oil mixture. By hand, with a mixer fitted with a dough hook or in the food processor fitted with the metal blade, stir the liquid into the flour mixture to form a soft dough. Add more flour until dough is still soft but does not stick to your hands. Knead for 10 minutes by hand, 5 minutes in a mixer or 1 minute in a food processor.
5. Place dough in a buttered bowl and turn around so that dough is com-
pletely buttered. Cover and allow to rise in a warm spot for 1 hour, or until doubled in bulk.
6. Punch dough down and knead in walnuts. Cut dough into two pieces and roll out each into a long oval shape approximately 14 x 6 inches (35 x 15 cm). Roll up lengthwise to form two long breads. Pinch seams closed.
7. Brush breads with lightly beaten egg white and roll in sesame seeds.
8. Place breads in two well-buttered French bread pans or on a large baking sheet. Cover loosely with buttered plastic wrap and allow to rise in a warm place until doubled in bulk, about 45 minutes.
9. Bake for 30 to 35 minutes in preheated 375°F (190°C) oven. Cool on racks immediately.

Caponata

I have been making this Sicilian eggplant spread for many years, but I never seem to tire of it. Use it as a relish with roasts or cold cuts, as a topping for pizzas or as a spread on toast or crackers. You can make up lots and freeze it; or it will keep for at least two weeks in the refrigerator.

Makes approximately 6 cups (1.5 L)

2	eggplants (2 lb/1 kg total)	2
1 tbsp	salt	15 mL
1/2 cup	extra-virgin olive oil	125 mL
2	onions, coarsely chopped	2
2	cloves garlic, finely chopped	2
pinch	hot red chili flakes	pinch
2	ribs celery, diced	2
1	28-oz (796 mL) tin plum tomatoes, pureed with juices	1
1 tbsp	capers	15 mL
2 tbsp	granulated sugar	25 mL
1/4 cup	red wine vinegar	50 mL
	Salt and freshly ground black pepper to taste	
1/2 cup	pine nuts, toasted	125 mL
1/2 cup	chopped fresh parsley	125 mL

1. Trim eggplants and cut into 1/2-inch (1 cm) dice. Toss with salt and place in colander set over another bowl. Allow to rest for 30 minutes until the salt draws any bitter liquid out of eggplant. Squeeze eggplant cubes gently and discard any liquid.
2. In large deep skillet, heat 1/3 cup (75 mL) olive oil on medium-high heat. Add half the eggplant and cook until well browned on all sides, about 7 to 10 minutes. Remove and drain on paper towels. Cook second batch. Drain and reserve.
3. Discard any oil left in pan and wipe out pan. Add remaining olive oil and heat. Add onions, garlic and chili flakes and cook gently for 8 to 10 minutes, until wilted and very fragrant.
4. Add celery and tomatoes and bring to the boil.
5. Stir in eggplant and capers. Reduce heat and cook gently for 15 minutes.
6. Meanwhile, in small saucepan, cook sugar and vinegar together until sugar dissolves. Stir into eggplant mixture. Cook eggplant, uncovered, on medium heat, until thickened, about 20 to 30 minutes.
7. Taste and adjust seasoning with salt and pepper. Stir in pine nuts and parsley. Refrigerate and serve cold as a spread or relish.

A Lighter Side: Instead of frying eggplant, slice eggplant, salt, drain and arrange on a baking sheet in a single layer. Brush lightly with olive oil. Broil, watching closely, until browned on both sides. Dice. Use only 2 tbsp (25 mL) olive oil for cooking onions.

Cheddar Beer Spread

It is easy and much less expensive to make up your own cheese spreads rather than buying them in fancy food shops. Use this as a spread or a sandwich filling. It is also great on toast and lightly broiled. Or you can make little cheese "truffles" by forming the cold mixture into small balls and rolling them in toasted crushed pecans. These "truffles" are great for appetizers and perfect with fruit after a meal.

Green peppercorns are mild unripe peppercorn berries. They come in jars or cans, packed in brine.

Makes approximately 3 cups (750 mL)

1 lb	aged Cheddar cheese	500 g		1 tsp	Worcestershire sauce	5 mL
4 oz	cream cheese	125 g		1 tsp	green peppercorns, crushed	5 mL
1/2 cup	flat beer	125 mL				
1/4 cup	sour cream	50 mL		1/4 tsp	Tabasco sauce	1 mL
2 tbsp	grainy mustard	25 mL		1/4 tsp	freshly ground black pepper	1 mL
1	clove garlic, minced	1				

1. Grate Cheddar cheese and blend well with cream cheese.
2. Beat in remaining ingredients. Taste and adjust seasoning if necessary. Serve in attractive bowl with bread or crackers.

A Lighter Side: Use low-fat Cheddar and low-fat pressed cottage cheese in place of the aged Cheddar and cream cheese. Use low-fat unflavored yogurt instead of the sour cream. Substitute light beer for regular beer.

CHILIES   *There seem to be hundreds of varieties of chilies, and the names can be very confusing. Not only can each variety have a different name depending on whether it is fresh or dried, but the same chili can have different names in different countries.*

Generally, the smaller and more pointed the chili, the hotter it is. And the same kinds of chilies can vary greatly in terms of heat.

When a recipe calls for mild green chilies, I like to use fresh poblano chilies that have been roasted, peeled and chopped. If I cannot find poblanos, I sometimes substitute tinned mild green chilies, although the taste and texture aren't nearly as good.

When recipes call for a hot chili, I usually use jalapeño or serrano. They can be roasted and peeled, but they are so small that I often do not bother.

If you have sensitive skin, always wear plastic gloves or just cover your hands with plastic bags when you handle chilies. And, of course, never wipe your eyes or mouth with your chili fingers! The ribs inside are the hottest part, and because the seeds touch the ribs, they are hot, too. If you want a slightly milder taste, derib and seed the chilies instead of chopping them up whole. (A little mini chopper works well, as you do not have to handle them as much.)

Baked Chèvre with Tomato Salsa

When I went to Santa Fe a few years ago to learn more about Southwestern food, I was surprised to see so much goat cheese used. It was becoming so popular and trendy, it never occurred to me that it was indigenous to the Southwest and had been used there for centuries!

Serve this with corn chips for dipping. The mixture can also be spread on cornbread or crusty French or Italian bread.

Serves 8

6	large ripe tomatoes	6
1	clove garlic, minced	1
1/3 cup	chopped fresh chives or green onions	75 mL
1 cup	chopped fresh coriander	250 mL
4	jalapeño chilies, seeded and finely chopped (more or less to taste)	4
1/2 tsp	salt	2 mL
1/2 tsp	freshly ground black pepper	2 mL
1 tbsp	lime juice	15 mL
10 oz	chèvre (creamy mild goat cheese)	300 g

1. Core tomatoes and cut in half. Squeeze out seeds. Chop tomatoes finely.
2. Combine tomatoes with garlic, chives, coriander, chilies, salt, pepper and lime juice. Taste for seasoning. Place sauce in flat serving dish with a slight lip.
3. Cut cheese into rounds about 3/4 inch (2 cm) thick. Arrange on baking sheet.
4. Just before serving, preheat broiler. Broil cheese about 6 inches (15 cm) from heat until warm and slightly browned. This should only take 2 to 3 minutes. Lift hot cheese off baking sheet and place on sauce.

A Lighter Side: Instead of using just the goat cheese, cream together 5 oz (150 g) goat cheese with 5 oz (150 g) low-fat pressed cottage cheese. Shape into rounds and broil as instructed above.

Oriental Eggplant Spread

This spread has a mysterious, almost addictive quality. It is low in calories and tastes wonderful on sesame crackers, or it can be served as a sauce with lamb chops.

Makes approximately 1 1/2 cups (375 mL)

1	large eggplant (1 1/2 lb/750 g)	1	4	cloves garlic, finely chopped	4
2 tbsp	soy sauce	25 mL	1 tbsp	finely chopped fresh ginger root	15 mL
2 tbsp	brown sugar	25 mL	4	green onions, chopped	4
1 tsp	rice vinegar	5 mL	1/2 tsp	oriental chili paste	2 mL
1 tbsp	water	15 mL	1 tsp	oriental sesame oil	5 mL
2 tbsp	vegetable oil	25 mL			

1. Place eggplant in baking dish and pierce in a few places. Bake in a pre-heated 425°F (220°C) oven for 45 to 50 minutes, or until tender *(or microwave, see page 46)*. Cool. Peel eggplant and chop finely.
2. In small bowl, combine soy sauce with sugar, vinegar and water.
3. In wok or skillet, heat oil on medium-high heat. Add garlic, ginger, 2 tbsp (25 mL) green onions and chili paste. Cook for 30 seconds until fragrant.
4. Add soy sauce mixture and, when bubbling, add eggplant. Stir to combine well. Heat thoroughly.
5. Remove from heat and stir in sesame oil. Place in serving bowl and sprinkle with remaining green onions. Serve cold or at room temperature.

Lobster Pâté with Caviar

This is a very elegant starter for a fancy dinner, or it can be a posh addition to a number of appetizers served at a cocktail party. Although caviar and lobster are both fairly expensive, you do get a lot of mileage out of them in this recipe. I like to use the frozen canned lobster meat (I think it has more flavor than frozen lobster tails). Just be sure to squeeze out excess moisture. You could also use cooked crab or baby shrimp.

Makes approximately 40 appetizers

12 oz	cooked lobster meat	375 g
3	hard-cooked eggs	3
1/4 cup	mayonnaise	50 mL
1 tbsp	chopped fresh dill	15 mL
1 tbsp	lemon juice	15 mL
1 tsp	Russian-style mustard	5 mL
1/4 tsp	freshly ground black pepper	1 mL
8	Belgian endives	8
1 oz	salmon or sturgeon caviar	30 g
1	bunch chives	1

1. Pat lobster dry. Chop into very small pieces. Reserve in large bowl.
2. Chop eggs and add to lobster.
3. In separate bowl, combine mayonnaise with dill, lemon juice, mustard and pepper.
4. Combine dressing with lobster or partially puree everything together in food processor.
5. Separate endive leaves, wash and pat dry. Spoon a little pâté into broad end of each endive leaf. Spoon a drop of caviar on each. Cut chives to fit the length of each endive and place one or two pieces of chive on each. Arrange on serving platter and garnish platter with fresh flowers.

A Lighter Side: Use low-fat unflavored yogurt in place of mayonnaise; use only hard-cooked egg whites and discard the yolks.

Mystery Dip

My friends Sharon, Lois and Bram are one of North America's top children's groups. They are always amazed to find that recipes are like songs — you find the same basic number all over the country with little regional variations. This is one of the recipes they have tasted from Toronto to Santa Fe. In Toronto, it is often served in a hollowed-out round loaf of dark rye bread, with thin slices of rye alongside for dipping. In Philadelphia, it is served in a crock accompanied by toasted pita bread. And for a Santa Fe version, fill miniature baked tartlet shells with the dip.

Makes approximately 2 1/2 cups (625 mL)

1 cup	mayonnaise	250 mL
1 cup	sour cream	250 mL
1	package dry vegetable soup mix (about 3 oz/90 g)	1
1	10-oz (300 g) package frozen chopped spinach, defrosted	1

1. Combine mayonnaise and sour cream. Stir in vegetable soup mix.
2. Squeeze any excess water from defrosted spinach. Chop finely if desired and stir into mayonnaise mixture.

A Lighter Side: Use low-fat mayonnaise and low-fat sour cream or unflavored yogurt.

PITA CHIPS *There are many pita chips available commercially, but none taste as good as those you make yourself.*

To make pita chips, just buy regular or whole wheat pita bread and split each pita into two rounds. Brush with melted butter or olive oil and sprinkle with herbs, salt, pepper, sesame seeds, poppy seeds or anything you wish. (For a low-fat version, use lightly beaten egg white instead of butter or oil.)

Cut each round into sixths and place on an ungreased baking sheet in a single layer. Bake in a preheated 350°F (180°C) oven for 8 to 10 minutes, or until browned and crisp. Serve warm, or cool and store in tins.

Smoked Salmon Tartare

Everyone loves smoked salmon appetizers, and this is a great one to add to your collection. You can use leftover pieces of smoked salmon or even scraps that you can often buy less expensively at fish markets.

Serve the tartare in an attractive bowl and allow guests to spread it on black bread, crackers or buttered toast. Or spread it on buttered black bread and arrange on a platter. The mixture can also be used to fill Belgian endive leaves or the scooped-out centers of thick cucumber slices *(page 23)*. Or it can be used as a topping on tiny corn pancakes or as a filling in Beggar's Purses *(page 71)*.

Makes approximately 2 1/2 cups (625 mL)

1 1/2 lb	smoked salmon	750 g
1/4 cup	extra-virgin olive oil	50 mL
1/3 cup	lime juice or lemon juice	75 mL
1/2 tsp	grated lime or lemon peel	2 mL
1/4 cup	chopped fresh chives or green onions	50 mL
1/4 cup	chopped fresh parsley	50 mL
1/4 cup	chopped fresh dill or basil	50 mL
1/2 tsp	Tabasco sauce	2 mL
2 tbsp	capers	25 mL
1/2 tsp	freshly ground black pepper	2 mL

1. Trim salmon if necessary. Chop coarsely.
2. Combine remaining ingredients in bowl. Add salmon and toss until very well combined. Taste and adjust seasoning if necessary.

A Lighter Side: Omit the olive oil.

Avocado Spread with Lime

It's hard to find ripe avocados the day you need them, so buy them a few days in advance and let them ripen on the counter. Once they are ripe, refrigerate them.

Makes 3 cups (750 mL)

8 oz	chèvre (creamy mild goat cheese) or ricotta cheese	250 g	1/2 tsp	freshly ground black pepper	2 mL
2	cloves garlic, minced	2	1/4 cup	lime juice	50 mL
2 tsp	chopped fresh rosemary (or 1/2 tsp/2 mL dried)	10 mL	4	small ripe avocados (or 2 large)	4
2 tsp	chopped fresh thyme (or 1/2 tsp/2 mL dried)	10 mL	1/2 tsp	Tabasco sauce	2 mL
1/3 cup	chopped fresh parsley	75 mL	1/2 tsp	salt	2 mL
1/4 tsp	hot red chili flakes	1 mL	1/4 cup	chopped fresh coriander or parsley	50 mL

1. In bowl, mash cheese roughly with a fork. Mash in garlic, rosemary, thyme, parsley, chili flakes, pepper and half the lime juice.
2. Cut each avocado in half, one at a time. Remove the pit. Holding the fruit in your hand with the skin next to your palm, gently slice the avocado, being sure not to go through the skin. Now slice it in the other direction. Gently remove the now diced flesh with a spoon. Add to the cheese. Repeat with the remaining avocados.

   Gently mash mixture together if you want it to be coarse. (This can all be done in a food processor, but the texture will be creamier.) Add remaining lime juice or more if necessary. Season with Tabasco sauce, salt and coriander to taste.
3. Cover with plastic wrap pressed directly on surface of the mixture. Refrigerate until ready to serve.

A Lighter Side: Use low-fat pressed cottage cheese instead of chèvre or ricotta.

Gorgonzola Pâté

Use a fresh creamy Gorgonzola or other mild creamy blue cheese for the best results. Serve this spread with rye bread or crusty Italian bread, or Walnut Bread with Sesame Seeds *(page 12)*.

Makes 1 1/2 cups (375 mL)

8 oz	Gorgonzola cheese	250 g	1/2 tsp	dried tarragon	2 mL
4 oz	cream cheese	125 g	1/4 tsp	freshly ground black	1 mL
1/2 cup	unsalted butter	125 mL		pepper	
2 tbsp	sour cream	25 mL	1/2 cup	chopped toasted walnuts	125 mL

1. In blender, food processor or electric mixer, blend Gorgonzola with cream cheese and butter. Stir in sour cream, tarragon and pepper. Stir in nuts.
2. Taste and adjust seasoning if necessary. Refrigerate until ready to serve. Allow mixture to rest at room temperature for 10 minutes before serving.

A Lighter Side: Use 8 oz (250 g) low-fat pressed cottage cheese in place of cream cheese and butter. Use low-fat unflavored yogurt instead of sour cream.

TOASTING NUTS *Nuts will have double or triple the flavor if they are toasted before you use them. And they are so expensive and high in fat, it is worth the trouble. Spread the nuts in a single layer on a baking sheet and bake in a preheated 350°F (180°C) oven for 5 to 10 minutes, until lightly browned. You can also toast a small quantity in a toaster oven or in the microwave. In the microwave, toast nuts 1/2 cup (125 mL) at a time in a glass dish for 50 to 70 seconds on High (100%) power. Cool before using.*

If you are sprinkling the nuts over something that will be baked, the nuts will toast anyway, so there is no need to pre-toast them.

Smoked Salmon Pâté

This was one of the most popular recipes in the *CKFM Bonnie Stern Cookbook*. It is my version of the pâté sold in many fancy food shops and delis. No one can ever get enough of it.

Makes one 9 x 5-inch (2 L) loaf

1	envelope unflavored gelatin	1
1/4 cup	cold water	50 mL
12 oz	smoked salmon, diced	375 g
4 oz	cream cheese	125 g
1 cup	sour cream	250 mL
2 tbsp	lemon juice	25 mL
1 1/2 cups	whipping cream	375 mL
	Salt and freshly ground black pepper to taste	
10 oz	spinach, cooked and squeezed dry	300 g
4	vine leaves, rinsed and dried (optional)	4

1. Sprinkle gelatin over cold water in small saucepan. Allow to rest for 5 minutes. Heat gently and stir to dissolve gelatin.
2. Place smoked salmon in food processor fitted with metal blade. Process until salmon is coarsely chopped. Add cream cheese and blend until smooth. Add sour cream and blend in well. Blend in lemon juice.
3. Add gelatin to mixture in food processor and combine well.
4. In large bowl, whip cream until gentle peaks form. Add all but a few tablespoons of salmon mixture to the whipped cream and fold in gently but thoroughly. Taste and adjust seasoning with salt and pepper.
5. Add spinach to remaining salmon mixture in food processor and blend well. Taste this mixture and adjust seasoning.
6. Line a 9 x 5-inch (2 L) loaf pan with plastic wrap and place a few vine leaves in the bottom. Add half the salmon mixture and spread evenly. Spread all of spinach mixture over that. Top with remaining salmon mixture.
7. Cover with plastic wrap and refrigerate for at least 3 hours.
8. To serve, unmold onto a plate and decorate with lemon twists *(page 6)*, tomato roses *(page 4)*, smoked salmon roses *(page 5)* and/or watercress.

A Lighter Side: Use low-fat pressed cottage cheese instead of cream cheese. Use 2 cups (500 mL) low-fat unflavored yogurt instead of the sour cream and whipped cream.

Smoked Salmon and Ricotta Mousse

This is a super way to use up leftover bits of smoked salmon or make a small amount serve more people.

Makes approximately 30 appetizers

8 oz	smoked salmon, diced	250 g
1/2 cup	unsalted butter, diced	125 mL
1/2 cup	ricotta cheese, well drained	125 mL
2 tbsp	lemon juice	25 mL
1 tsp	white horseradish	5 mL

1/2 tsp	freshly ground black pepper	2 mL
1	English cucumber	1
2	Belgian endives	2
	Sprigs of fresh dill	

1. In a bowl, combine smoked salmon and butter. Beat in cheese. Add lemon juice, horseradish and pepper. Taste and add salt only if necessary.
2. Slice cucumber into 1/2-inch (1 cm) slices. Using a melon baller, scoop out centers but leave a thin layer in the middle for the base. Pat dry. Separate endive leaves.

3. Pipe or spoon mousse into center of each cucumber round and into end of each endive. Mousse can also be piped onto squares of black bread.
4. Garnish each appetizer with a sprig of fresh dill. Refrigerate but allow to come to room temperature for about 10 minutes before serving.

A Lighter Side: Use 8 oz (250 g) low-fat pressed cottage cheese in place of the butter and ricotta.

Marinated Chèvre with Black Olives

Even people who do not think they really like the tanginess of chèvre like this dish. Serve it with crackers, French bread and/or mini pitas. Guests can scoop up some of the cheese and a little of the oil on the bread or crackers.

Makes 1 lb (500 g)

1 lb	chèvre (creamy mild goat cheese)	500 g
2	cloves garlic, cut in half and smashed	2
2 tbsp	chopped fresh rosemary (or 1/2 tsp/2 mL dried)	25 mL
2 tbsp	chopped fresh thyme (or 1/2 tsp/2 mL dried)	25 mL
1 tbsp	chopped fresh parsley	15 mL
2 tbsp	chopped fresh basil	25 mL
1/4 tsp	hot red chili flakes	1 mL
1 tsp	whole black peppercorns (or 1/4 tsp/1 mL freshly ground)	5 mL
1/2 cup	pitted and chopped black olives (preferably Kalamata)	125 mL
1/4 cup	chopped sun-dried tomatoes	50 mL
1 cup	extra-virgin olive oil	250 mL

1. Slice cheese into rounds 1 inch (2.5 cm) thick. Arrange in one layer in serving dish.
2. Place garlic pieces around cheese (remove them later).
3. Sprinkle cheese with herbs, chili flakes, peppercorns, olives and tomatoes. Cover with olive oil.
4. Cover and allow to marinate for a few hours at room temperature or in the refrigerator for a few days. Remove garlic and allow cheese to come to room temperature before serving.

A Lighter Side: Blend 8 oz (250 g) chèvre with 8 oz (250 g) low-fat pressed cottage cheese and then shape into rounds as above. You will lose some of the flavor of the chèvre, but will have a dish with less fat. Drain cheese well before serving.

Baked Chèvre with Pesto Vinaigrette

Not only can this be served as a spread, it is also wonderful as a topping on a bed of mixed greens (if you are serving it as a topping on a salad, make the rounds of cheese smaller).

Serves 8 to 10

1 cup	packed fresh basil leaves	250 mL
1/4 cup	packed fresh parsley leaves	50 mL
2 tbsp	chopped fresh chives	25 mL
2	cloves garlic, minced	2
1/3 cup	pine nuts, toasted	75 mL
1/4 cup	balsamic or red wine vinegar	50 mL
1/2 cup	extra-virgin olive oil	125 mL
1/2 tsp	salt	2 mL
1/4 tsp	freshly ground black pepper	1 mL
1 lb	chèvre (creamy mild goat cheese)	500 g
2 cups	fresh breadcrumbs	500 mL

1. Chop basil, parsley and chives finely by hand or in food processor.
2. Add garlic and pine nuts. Combine briefly. (If doing this by hand, you may want to chop pine nuts slightly first.)
3. Blend in vinegar and oil. Season with salt and pepper.
4. Cut cheese into rounds 1 inch (2.5 cm) thick. Pat crumbs on both sides. Place cheese on baking sheet brushed with olive oil.
5. Just before serving, bake cheese in a preheated 400°F (200°C) oven for 3 to 5 minutes, or until just beginning to melt. Watch cheese closely.
6. Transfer hot cheese rounds to serving dish in a single layer and spoon pesto around. Serve with bread or crackers.

A Lighter Side: Use half the amount of pine nuts in the pesto and substitute water for half the olive oil. For an even leaner version, blend 8 oz (250 g) chèvre with 8 oz (250 g) low-fat pressed cottage cheese and shape into rounds before dipping into breadcrumbs.

HOMEMADE BREADCRUMBS *Make fresh homemade breadcrumbs from bread that is not dried out, but not necessarily "fresh." Break the bread into chunks and process on/off in a food processor until you have coarse crumbs. (If I am using the crumbs for breading foods, I do not use the crusts, as they tend to burn.) Store the crumbs in the freezer, since they are still somewhat moist and will go moldy at room temperature. Use them from the frozen state.*

To toast breadcrumbs, spread them on a baking sheet and bake in a preheated 350°F (180°C) oven for 5 to 10 minutes, or until brown. When they are completely dried out, they can be stored at room temperature.

Guacamole

Although I usually make guacamole differently every time, depending on the ingredients I happen to have on hand, I do always like a tiny bit of garlic and something a little spicy. And I like the texture to be coarse rather than finely pureed.

Try to add the avocados to the tomato mixture just before serving, but if you have to make it all ahead, don't worry. Just cover the mixture with plastic wrap placed directly on its surface. You can serve guacamole as a dip, as a sauce with grilled fish, chicken or lamb, or as a filling in chimichangas, tacos or burritos.

Makes approximately 2 1/2 cups (625 mL)

1	small ripe tomato, seeded and finely chopped	1	1/4 tsp	freshly ground black pepper	1 mL
1	clove garlic, minced	1	1/4 cup	lime juice	50 mL
1	jalapeño chili, seeded and finely chopped	1	3	small ripe avocados, (or 2 large avocados)	3
1/2 tsp	salt	2 mL	1/4 cup	chopped fresh coriander	50 mL

1. In bowl, combine tomato, garlic, jalapeño, salt, pepper and lime juice. Reserve this mixture.
2. Just before serving, peel and dice avocados *(page 20)* and combine with tomato mixture and coriander, mashing avocados slightly so that mixture will spread well. Serve with yellow and blue corn chips for a dip, or spread on round yellow corn chips topped with sour cream and caviar.

AVOCADOS   *If possible, buy the "ugly" dark-green Haas avocados rather than the large light-green ones. The small ones are more buttery and less watery.*

Pesto and Mascarpone Torte

This layered cheese spread is a spectacular company treat. Serve it with crackers or French bread. Any leftovers can easily be used as a sandwich filling, and I have even tossed this mixture with fettuccine, a little butter and Parmesan for a sensational pasta dish.

Mascarpone is a creamy Italian cheese that is increasingly available in North America. It is used in a traditional Italian dessert called "tiramisu" that is fast becoming one of the most popular desserts of all time! If you cannot find it, substitute 12 oz (375 g) cream cheese blended with 1/2 cup (125 mL) unsalted butter.

You can make different tortas by layering the cheese with other mixtures such as Olivada *(page 28)*.

In this recipe, if fresh basil is not available, use fresh parsley.

Serves 8 to 10

PESTO

2	cloves garlic	2
2 cups	packed fresh basil leaves	500 mL
1/3 cup	pine nuts, lightly toasted	75 mL
1/2 cup	freshly grated Parmesan cheese (preferably Parmigiano Reggiano)	125 mL
1/4 cup	extra-virgin olive oil	50 mL
1/2 tsp	salt	2 mL
1/2 tsp	freshly ground black pepper	2 mL
1 lb	mascarpone cheese	500 g
1/4 cup	thinly sliced sun-dried tomatoes or black olives (preferably Kalamata)	50 mL

1. In food processor or blender, puree garlic with basil, pine nuts and Parmesan cheese. Drizzle in olive oil. Season with salt and pepper. Reserve.
2. In bowl, cream mascarpone and reserve.
3. Line a 4-cup (1 L) soufflé dish, Charlotte mold or loaf pan with plastic wrap. Spread one-quarter of the mascarpone in bottom. Top with one-third of the pesto mixture. Sprinkle one-third of the tomatoes on pesto. Repeat layers, ending with cheese.
4. Cover with plastic wrap and refrigerate for a few hours or overnight.
5. To serve, unmold onto serving dish and decorate with fresh basil leaves or additional sun-dried tomatoes.

A Lighter Side: Instead of using mascarpone, use low-fat pressed cottage cheese and process it in a food processor until smooth. Use 2 tbsp (25 mL) olive oil in the pesto instead of 1/4 cup (50 mL). The taste and texture of the torte will be very different, but still good.

Smoked Trout Mousse

This is so easy but tastes so good — the kind of recipe that every cook loves to have on hand. You can serve it as a spread with black, rye or French bread, or use it as a stuffing for vegetables such as Belgian endive, mushroom caps or cucumber rings *(page 23)*.

Makes approximately 1 1/2 cups (375 mL)

3	whole smoked trout (about 8 oz/250 g each)	3		2 tbsp	chopped fresh dill	25 mL
1/3 cup	mayonnaise	75 mL		2 tbsp	chopped fresh chives or green onions	25 mL
1 tbsp	white horseradish	15 mL		1/2 tsp	freshly ground black pepper	2 mL
3 tbsp	lemon juice	50 mL				

1. Fillet trout and remove as many bones as possible. You should have about 12 oz (375 g) filleted trout. Chop finely by hand or in food processor.

2. Blend in remaining ingredients and adjust seasonings to taste.

A Lighter Side: Use low-fat mayonnaise or unflavored yogurt instead of the mayonnaise.

Olivada

This heady mixture is great spread on pita bread or toast, but it is also wonderful as a topping for swordfish or lamb chops, or as a condiment in roast beef sandwiches.

Makes approximately 1 1/2 cups (375 mL)

1	clove garlic, minced	1		1/2 tsp	freshly ground black pepper	2 mL
3 tbsp	finely chopped red onion	50 mL		1/3 cup	unsalted butter	75 mL
3 tbsp	finely chopped fresh basil or parsley	50 mL				
2 cups	black olives (preferably Kalamata), pitted and coarsely chopped	500 mL				

1. Combine garlic, onion, basil and olives in food processor or blender.
2. Beat in pepper and butter. Taste and adjust seasoning with salt and pepper.

A Lighter Side: Omit butter and use 1 tbsp (15 mL) olive oil instead.

Cream Cheese Spread with Herbs

This is a homemade version of herb cream cheese. You can vary the mixture by adding leftover bits of cheese or by using chèvre instead of cream cheese. Serve it with bread or crackers, use it as a topping on baked potatoes, or pipe the cheese into Belgian endive leaves, hollowed-out mushrooms or cherry tomatoes. You can also thin the cheese with additional sour cream to use as a dip with vegetables.

Use this cheese in any recipe that calls for Rondele or Boursin.

Makes approximately 1 cup (250 mL)

8 oz	cream cheese	250 g	1 tsp	chopped fresh thyme (or pinch dried)	5 mL
1/4 cup	sour cream or unflavored yogurt	50 mL	1/4 tsp	salt	1 mL
1	clove garlic, minced	1	1/4 tsp	freshly ground black pepper	1 mL
1/4 cup	chopped fresh parsley	50 mL	1/4 tsp	Tabasco sauce	1 mL
2 tbsp	chopped fresh chives or green onions	25 mL			
1 tbsp	chopped fresh tarragon (or 1/2 tsp/2 mL dried)	15 mL			

1. In food processor, blender or electric mixer, whip cream cheese and sour cream together until smooth and well combined.
2. Add remaining ingredients. Taste and adjust seasonings if necessary.

A Lighter Side: Use ricotta or low-fat pressed cottage cheese instead of the cream cheese. Use low-fat sour cream or unflavored yogurt instead of the regular sour cream.

HERBS   *Until recently, only fine restaurants and hotel dining rooms had access to a wide selection of fresh herbs year round. (I think that was one of the biggest advantages that restaurants had over home cooking.) Now more and more fresh herbs are becoming available to home cooks. They are worth even a terrible price in winter, as they make your food sing.*

When using leafy fresh herbs like parsley, coriander, basil, dill and tarragon, I am extremely generous. I am slightly more cautious with fresh rosemary and thyme, as they are a little more potent, but when I am using dried herbs I am extremely careful. They become strong and bitter easily and I never follow the standard rule found in most cookbooks that you should use one-third the amount of dried herbs as fresh. When I have fresh herbs, I use lots. When I have dried herbs I use a small amount.

Wash fresh herbs and then dry them well. Wrap in a tea towel and place in a plastic bag. Store in the refrigerator. Basil is extremely delicate, so I usually wrap it especially well, as it begins to discolor at low temperatures.

Herbed Crab Dip with Pita

Pita bread is great to serve with dips because the bread is firm and easy to manipulate into tiny cups. If you can find the tiny pita breads, cut them in half and the pockets will be perfect for dipping!

Serves 8

4 oz	herb cream cheese (e.g. Boursin or Rondele, or *see page 29*)	125 g
1/3 cup	mayonnaise	75 mL
1/3 cup	sour cream	75 mL
3 1/2 oz	frozen snow crab, defrosted, picked over and shredded, with excess liquid squeezed out	100 g
1/4 tsp	freshly ground black pepper	1 mL
1 tbsp	lemon juice	15 mL
12	mini pita breads	12

1. In food processor, blender or electric mixer, beat cheese, mayonnaise and sour cream until creamy.
2. Squeeze crab again to drain off any remaining liquid. Stir crab into cheese.
3. Add pepper and lemon juice. Taste and adjust seasoning if necessary.
4. Serve with mini pita breads cut in half, or cut a large pita into 2-inch (5 cm) pieces.

A Lighter Side: Make A Lighter Side version of Cream Cheese Spread with Herbs (page 29) and use in place of the herb cream cheese listed above. Use low-fat mayonnaise or unflavored yogurt instead of the mayonnaise; use low-fat sour cream or more unflavored yogurt instead of the sour cream.

HOMEMADE MAYONNAISE   *If your homemade mayonnaise does not thicken, don't worry. Just pour the thin mayonnaise into a measuring cup. Rinse and dry the blender or food processor and add a room temperature egg yolk. With the machine running, very slowly dribble the thin sauce into the yolk. The mixture should come together and thicken.*

Aioli with Vegetables

When garlic is cooked for a long time, it becomes gentle and sweet-tasting, quite unlike the strong, direct taste of raw garlic. In this recipe the raw garlic flavor is rich and vibrant. The dip can be spooned into fish stews for a last-minute burst of flavor, used as a sauce for fish or chicken, or as a spread for sandwiches made with cold cuts.

You can serve this on a large platter with drinks, or you can lay out individual portions on salad plates or in small baskets. For individual servings, use a Chinese tea cup or small vegetable such as an artichoke or cucumber flower (*page 5*) to hold the dip.

Serves 8 to 10

1 lb	asparagus	500 g
1	bunch broccoli	1
1 lb	carrots	500 g
8 oz	green beans	250 g
1	large bulb fennel	1
2	Belgian endives	2
1	red cabbage	1

AIOLI		
2	cloves garlic	2
2 tbsp	lemon juice	25 mL
1 tbsp	white wine vinegar	15 mL
2	egg yolks	2
1/4 tsp	Tabasco sauce	1 mL
1 tsp	Dijon mustard	5 mL
1/2 tsp	salt	2 mL
1/4 tsp	freshly ground black pepper	1 mL
1 1/4 cups	extra-virgin olive oil	300 mL

1. Break tough ends off asparagus. Peel an inch or two up stalks. Cook in boiling water until tender-crisp, 3 to 5 minutes. Rinse with cold water and pat dry.
2. Trim tough ends from broccoli. Cut into pieces with florets on stems for easier dipping. Cook in boiling water for 2 to 3 minutes until tender-crisp. Rinse with cold water and pat dry.
3. Peel and trim carrots and cut into 2-inch (5 cm) sticks. If carrots are thick, cut in half lengthwise. Cook in boiling water for 3 to 4 minutes until tender-crisp, rinse with cold water and pat dry.
4. Trim beans. Cook in boiling water for 2 to 3 minutes until tender-crisp, rinse with cold water and pat dry.
5. Cut fennel into sticks. Break apart Belgian endives.
6. Cut red cabbage in half. Hollow out one half to hold dip and use the insides and other half in another recipe.
7. Arrange vegetables attractively on large platter.
8. Prepare aioli by placing garlic in blender or food processor. Add lemon juice, vinegar, egg yolks, Tabasco, mustard, salt and pepper. Blend. Add 1/4 cup (50 mL) oil. With machine running, add remaining oil slowly through feed tube until mayonnaise is as thick is you wish (more oil will give you a thicker mayonnaise). Taste and adjust seasoning if necessary.
9. Spoon aioli into hollowed-out cabbage and arrange in center of vegetables.

A Lighter Side: For aioli, omit egg yolks, olive oil and salt and combine remaining ingredients with 3/4 cup (175 mL) low-fat mayonnaise and 3/4 cup (175 mL) low-fat unflavored yogurt.

Country Pâté

Linda Stephen developed this pâté for our French Provincial cooking class. It is a traditional pâté that is always a big hit! Serve it with French stick and cornichons.

Serves 8 to 10

12 oz	lean pork	375 g
12 oz	lean veal	375 g
4 oz	pork fat	125 g
8 oz	calves liver	250 g
2 tbsp	unsalted butter	25 mL
1	onion, finely chopped	1
2	cloves garlic, finely chopped	2
1	egg, beaten	1
2 tbsp	Cognac or brandy	25 mL
1 1/2 tsp	salt	7 mL
1/2 tsp	freshly ground black pepper	2 mL
1/4 tsp	dried savory	1 mL
1/4 tsp	dried thyme	1 mL
1/4 tsp	grated nutmeg	1 mL
1/4 tsp	ground cloves	1 mL
12 oz	Black Forest ham, thickly sliced	375 g
1	bay leaf	1

1. Have butcher grind together pork, veal and pork fat. (Otherwise grind meat at home.) Puree liver in food processor. Combine all meat in large bowl.
2. In small saucepan, melt butter on medium-high heat. Cook onion and garlic for a few minutes until fragrant and tender.
3. Add onion mixture to meat along with egg, Cognac and seasonings. Mix together well.
4. Cut ham into julienne strips.
5. Butter a 6-cup (1.5 L) pâté mold or loaf pan and line with parchment paper. Butter again. Place one-quarter of meat mixture in bottom of pan. Cover with one-third of ham strips. Repeat layers, ending with meat. Top with bay leaf.
6. Cover terrine with double thickness of foil. Bake in a water bath (*see below*) in a preheated 350°F (180°C) oven for 1 1/2 hours.
7. Remove from water bath. Weight loaf with heavy object. Refrigerate overnight for best flavor and texture.

BAIN-MARIE   *For some reason, people seem to be intimidated when recipes call for a bain marie or water bath. But a bain-marie is really just a way of cooking foods gently so that the texture is creamy and tender. Pâtés, soufflés and pudding-like desserts such as crème caramel are often cooked in a bain-marie.*

Place the dish containing the prepared food in a larger pan. Pour very hot tap water into the larger pan until the water reaches halfway up the sides of the baking dish that contains the food. (It is usually easier to pour the water in after the dishes are in the oven.)

Black Bean Pesto

This spread can also be made with red kidney beans or chickpeas. Serve it as a dip with yellow and blue corn chips.

Makes approximately 3 cups (750 mL)

2 cups	canned or cooked black turtle beans *(page 154)*	500 mL	1/2 tsp	cayenne pepper	2 mL
2	cloves garlic, minced	2	4 oz	chèvre (creamy mild goat cheese), crumbled	125 g
3 tbsp	lime juice	50 mL	1/2 cup	cooked or frozen corn niblets (about 1 ear)	125 mL
3 tbsp	extra-virgin olive oil	50 mL	1/2 cup	chopped fresh coriander	125 mL
1 tsp	ground cumin	5 mL		Salt and freshly ground black pepper to taste	
1 tbsp	ground coriander	15 mL			

1. Drain beans well. Chop coarsely in food processor fitted with metal blade and add garlic, lime juice and olive oil. Process until semi-pureed.
2. Add cumin, ground coriander and cayenne and process briefly.

3. Stir in cheese, corn and fresh coriander. Taste and add salt and pepper if necessary.

A Lighter Side: Instead of the olive oil, use water. Omit the cheese.

DRIED BEANS AND LENTILS *Lentils can be used in salads, soups and casseroles. The pink (sometimes called red or orange) are tiny, so I use them in soups or in dishes where I don't mind if they lose their shape. They cook quickly and often do not need to be pureed. For salads and casseroles, I usually use the larger, firmer green (sometimes called brown) lentils. They take a bit longer to cook but hold their shape. Rinse lentils before using, and pick them over, since they can contain foreign particles like tiny stones.*

Like lentils, split peas do not need soaking, and they cook more quickly than most beans.

White kidney beans and black turtle beans used to require overnight soaking, but now I usually only soak them for a few hours. I then cover them with a lot of cold water and cook them (without salt) until tender. (Diana Kennedy, the world authority on Mexican cooking, does not soak these beans and recommends cooking them in a slow cooker.)

I find that chickpeas still need soaking overnight and usually take a longer time to cook than other beans. Pressure cookers are making a big comeback and can be used to cook beans. Be sure to follow the manufacturer's instructions.

Chicken Liver Pâté with Peppercorns

This is a creamy spread with lots of peppercorns. Serve it with crackers or egg bread.

If you make the aspic for the top, the pâté will look very professional and elegant, but you can also just sprinkle the crushed peppercorns right on the surface of the pâté — not as elegant, but equally delicious. To crush the peppercorns coarsely you can use a spice mill, a pepper mill that has an adjustable grind, or use an old chef's trick — put the peppercorns in a paper bag and take them outside. With the heaviest saucepan or skillet you have, bang them like mad on the pavement! It works every time.

Serves 8 to 10

1/4 cup	unsalted butter	50 mL
2	onions, chopped	2
2	cloves garlic, finely chopped	2
1 1/2 lb	chicken livers, trimmed and halved	750 g
1 tsp	salt	5 mL
1/4 tsp	freshly ground black pepper	1 mL
1 tsp	curry powder	5 mL
1/4 cup	Port	50 mL

1/4 cup	Cognac or brandy	50 mL
3/4 cup	whipping cream	175 mL

GLAZE

1 cup	chicken stock	250 mL
2 tbsp	Port, Cognac or brandy	25 mL
1	envelope unflavored gelatin	1
2 tbsp	coarsely ground black peppercorns	25 mL
2 tbsp	coarsely ground white peppercorns	25 mL

1. Melt butter in large skillet on medium-high heat. Add onions and garlic and cook until tender and fragrant, about 8 to 10 minutes.
2. Add chicken livers and cook until colored and cooked through to a pink color inside.
3. Transfer livers and onions to food processor. Add salt, pepper and curry powder. Blend until coarsely chopped. Reserve.
4. Add Port and Cognac to skillet and cook, stirring constantly, to scrape up any bits of liver and onions stuck to bottom of the pan. Cook for 2 minutes until slightly reduced. Add to livers and blend in briefly.
5. Blend in cream. Pour mixture (do not worry if it is runny) into a buttered 8-inch (2 L) square baking dish. Bake in a preheated 350°F (180°C) oven for 20 minutes. Cool completely.
6. For glaze, combine chicken stock with Port in small saucepan. Sprinkle with gelatin. Allow to rest for 5 minutes. Heat gently on low heat until gelatin just dissolves. Cool slightly — about 5 minutes.
7. Sprinkle peppercorns over surface of the cooled pâté. Pour on cooled gelatin mixture very carefully. Refrigerate until cold.

A Lighter Side: Omit cream, use half the amount of Port and Cognac in pâté, and do not bake. Simply put pureed mixture in a bowl for spreading on crackers or bread. The glaze can be omitted if you wish.

3

Hors d'oeuvre

Pepper Gougère

Mary Risely, my friend in San Francisco who owns the Tante Marie School of Cooking, shared this recipe with me.

Gougère is a cream puff pastry with cheese and herbs. It is a dish from Burgundy that was originally enjoyed with Burgundy wines, but now it is enjoyed any time.

Serves 6 to 8

1/2 cup	unsalted butter, diced	125 mL
1 cup	water	250 mL
1 cup	all-purpose flour	250 mL
4	eggs	4
1 tsp	Dijon mustard	5 mL
1/2 tsp	dry mustard	2 mL
1 1/2 cups	grated Gruyère cheese (about 6 oz/175 g)	375 mL
1 tbsp	freshly ground black pepper, or more to taste	15 mL
1 1/2 tsp	salt	7 mL
2 tbsp	freshly grated Parmesan cheese (preferably Parmigiano Reggiano)	25 mL

1. Place butter and water in saucepan over low heat until butter melts. Bring to a boil.
2. Remove pan from heat and add flour all at once. Stir quickly until dough comes together to form a ball. Return to medium heat and cook until dough dries out a bit, smearing dough along bottom of pan with a wooden spoon. Remove from heat and transfer dough to mixing bowl. Cool for about 5 minutes.
3. Beat in eggs one at a time. Mixture will be quite slippery. (You can use a hand mixer if you prefer, or even a food processor.) Beat in mustards, Gruyère, pepper and salt.
4. Line baking sheet with parchment paper. For individual puffs, spoon mixture in 2 tbsp (25 mL) mounds about 2 inches (5 cm) apart. Or, for a golden crown shape, form larger mounds into a ring. Sprinkle with grated Parmesan.
5. Bake in a preheated 425°F (220°C) oven for about 25 to 35 minutes depending on size, or until puffed and browned. Turn off oven. Pierce each mound with the point of a sharp knife to allow steam to escape. Return to turned-off oven for 10 to 15 minutes.

A Lighter Side: Use only 1/4 cup (50 mL) butter and 3/4 cup (175 mL) grated Gruyère cheese.

Southwest Salmon Cakes with Chipotle Mayonnaise

These bite-sized patties just burst with the flavor of the Southwest. You can make them with scallops or shrimp if you prefer. You can also serve three of these with the mayonnaise as a sit-down first course.

Makes 25 small patties

5 tbsp	unsalted butter	75 mL
2	cloves garlic, finely chopped	2
1	serrano chili, chopped	1
1	sweet red pepper, roasted, peeled, seeded and diced	1
1 cup	cooked or frozen corn niblets (about 2 ears)	250 mL
1/3 cup	chopped fresh coriander	75 mL
1 lb	fresh salmon fillets, cold	500 g

2	egg whites, cold	2
1/3 cup	whipping cream, cold	75 mL
1 tsp	salt	5 mL
1/4 tsp	freshly ground black pepper	1 mL
4 oz	smoked salmon, diced	125 g

CHIPOTLE MAYONNAISE

2 to 4	chipotle chilies (tinned)	2 to 4
1 cup	mayonnaise	250 mL

1. Melt 2 tbsp (25 mL) butter in skillet on medium-high heat. Add garlic, serrano chili and red pepper. Cook for a few minutes until fragrant. Cool.
2. In large bowl, combine red pepper mixture with corn and coriander.
3. Remove skin from salmon and trim. Cut into 1-inch (2.5 cm) pieces. Place in food processor fitted with the metal blade and chop coarsely. Add egg whites and puree. Blend in whipping cream, salt and pepper.
4. Add salmon-cream mixture and smoked salmon to corn mixture. Stir in. Shape into about 25 small patties. Place on a waxed paper-lined baking sheet. (Refrigerate for up to 12 hours if not cooking right away.)
5. To cook, melt remaining 3 tbsp (50 mL) butter in a large heavy (preferably non-stick) skillet on medium-high heat. Cook patties for 4 minutes per side until golden-brown and cooked through.
6. Meanwhile, in food processor, blend chipotle chilies until pureed. Stir in mayonnaise. (If mixture is too spicy, add unflavored yogurt or sour cream.) Serve with salmon cakes.

A Lighter Side: Use half the butter for cooking the peppers and later for cooking the patties (be sure to use a non-stick pan). Use milk instead of whipping cream when pureeing the salmon mixture. For the dip, use half low-fat mayonnaise and half low-fat unflavored yogurt.

CHIPOTLE CHILIES   *Chipotle chilies are smoked jalapeños. They are hot and have a unique smoky flavor. They are usually sold in tins and come packed in adobo sauce — a spicy tomato sauce. If you can not find chipotles, use jalapeños instead, though these will not give a smoky taste. Leftover chipotles can be frozen in their sauce in ice cube trays, or they will keep for several weeks in the refrigerator.*

Nachos

Nachos are great with the cheese alone, or after baking you can top them with diced mild chilies, diced hot jalapeños, chopped fresh coriander or parsley, or even diced avocado. They can also be dipped into refried beans, guacamole or sour cream as they are eaten.

Serves 6 to 8

3 cups	corn chips	750 mL
2 cups	grated Cheddar or Monterey Jack cheese (about 8 oz/250 g)	500 mL

1/2 cup	sour cream	125 mL
2 tbsp	chopped fresh coriander or parsley	25 mL

1. Arrange corn chips in a single layer on pizza pan or large ovenproof serving dish. Sprinkle with grated cheese.
2. Bake in a preheated 400°F (200°C) oven for 4 to 6 minutes, just until cheese melts and begins to bubble.
3. In small bowl, combine sour cream with the coriander to use for dipping.
4. Serve from the baking dish (children should be cautioned not to touch hot plate) with everyone pulling chips apart. Dip chips into sour cream mixture if desired.

A Lighter Side: Use low-fat mozzarella cheese. Use low-fat unflavored yogurt instead of sour cream for dipping.

FRESH CORIANDER *People either love or hate this zesty, citrus-tasting herb — the most used herb in the world. It is traditionally used in India, Thailand, China, Mexico, the Middle East and the Southwest, but I have even seen it used in France and Italy. Fresh coriander is also known as Chinese parsley and cilantro, depending on where you buy it. Although it is very distinctive and there is really no substitute, use other fresh herbs like parsley, mint or basil if you cannot find it or do not like it. Or, if you don't like it, try using just a little — you may get used to it!*

Although fresh coriander grows from coriander seed (used in curry powder), dried, powdered coriander has a very different flavor, and is no substitute for fresh coriander.

Smoked Salmon Tortilla Spirals

This is one of the most well-used appetizers I make in my classes. It's different, but not too different, and uses that ever popular ingredient, smoked salmon, in a way that does not require you to mortgage your house. If you are making these ahead, omit the Boston lettuce leaves, as they will get soggy if allowed to stand more than a few hours. Or use spinach instead, since it is sturdier.

A variation is to use a very creamy egg salad instead of the cream cheese. And children love the idea of these rolls, too. Fill them with tuna salad for lunch boxes.

Makes approximately 32 spirals

8 oz	cream cheese	250 g
2 tbsp	Russian-style mustard	25 mL
1 tbsp	mayonnaise or sour cream	15 mL
4	9-inch (23 cm) flour tortillas	4

12 oz	smoked salmon, thinly sliced	375 g
2 tbsp	chopped fresh dill	25 mL
2 tbsp	chopped fresh chives	25 mL
8	leaves Boston lettuce	8

1. Cream together cream cheese, mustard and mayonnaise.
2. Arrange tortillas on counter and spread evenly with cheese spread.
3. Arrange smoked salmon on top of cheese. Leave about 1-inch (2.5 cm) border at top covered just with cheese so that the rolls will adhere better. Sprinkle salmon with dill and chives. Arrange lettuce on top.

4. Roll tortillas up tightly, pressing firmly to seal. Wrap well and refrigerate until ready to serve. Trim off ends of rolls (eat them) and then cut each roll into 8 to 10 slices. Serve, spiral side up, on shredded lettuce.

A Lighter Side: Use low-fat pressed cottage cheese instead of cream cheese and low-fat unflavored yogurt instead of mayonnaise.

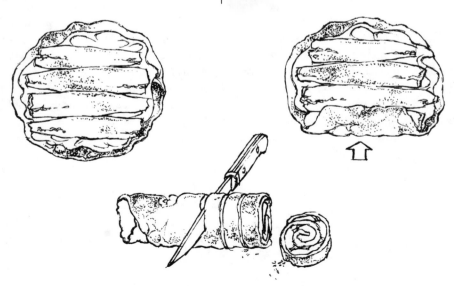

Spicy Wings with Blue Cheese Dip

The secret to crispy wings is to cook them with a dry spice mix — not a liquid marinade or sauce.

Makes approximately 40 pieces

3 lb	chicken wings (about 20)	1.5 kg
1 tsp	paprika	5 mL
1 tsp	dry mustard	5 mL
1/2 tsp	ground cumin	2 mL
1/2 tsp	salt	2 mL
1/4 tsp	freshly ground black pepper	1 mL
1/4 tsp	cayenne pepper	1 mL

BLUE CHEESE DIP

1/2 cup	mayonnaise	125 mL
1/2 cup	sour cream	125 mL
4 oz	blue cheese	125 g
1/2 tsp	dried tarragon	2 mL
1/2 tsp	Tabasco sauce	2 mL

1. Cut wings into three pieces. Freeze the wing tips for stock and pat the other pieces dry.
2. In a large bowl, combine the spices. Toss with wing pieces.
3. Arrange wings in a single layer on a rack set over a baking sheet. Bake in a preheated 425°F (220°C) oven for 20 minutes per side, or until very crisp.

4. Meanwhile, in a food processor or blender, combine mayonnaise, sour cream, blue cheese, tarragon and Tabasco. Serve wings with dip.

A Lighter Side: Use low-fat mayonnaise. Use low-fat unflavored yogurt instead of sour cream.

Smoked Salmon Sushi

This variation of sushi combines the Japanese technique with the Western flavors of dill and smoked salmon. For an even more European approach, try using 2 tbsp (25 mL) Russian-style mustard instead of the wasabi. You can also add a strip of blanched green onion or toasted sesame seeds with the salmon.

A sudari mat is a flexible bamboo mat (sometimes made of plastic now) that helps you roll up sushi. If you do not have one, Elizabeth Andoh, an authority on Japanese cooking, recommends using a pliable placemat.

Serves 8

1 1/2 cups	short-grain rice	375 mL
1 3/4 cups	cold water	425 mL
5 tbsp	sushi su (seasoned vinegar)	75 mL
4	large sheets pretoasted nori (dark dried laver)	4
1 tsp	wasabi (green horseradish)	5 mL
4 oz	smoked salmon, cut into strips	125 g
1/2	English cucumber, seeded and cut into strips	1/2
1	small bunch dill, blanched in boiling water for 30 seconds	1
1/2 cup	soy sauce	125 mL

1. Prepare rice by washing it until the water runs clear. Place in heavy saucepan with the cold water. Cover with tight-fitting lid and allow to rest for 15 minutes. Cook over high heat for 4 to 5 minutes while lid jumps up and down and rice bubbles and foams. Reduce heat to medium and cook for 8 to 10 minutes. Remove from heat and allow rice to rest for 15 minutes to steam. Do not remove lid at any time.
2. When rice is ready, place in wooden bowl and toss gently while sprinkling with sushi su vinegar. Fan rice dry at the same time. Divide rice into four equal portions.
3. Place one sheet of nori on a sudari mat with the bumpy side up. Top with portion of rice. Dampen hands with cold water and spread rice right to the edges of the nori, but leave 1/2 inch (1 cm) at the top. Combine wasabi with a tiny bit of water to make a paste and spread a little across the middle of rice.
4. Cover wasabi with one or two strips of salmon, cucumber and dill. Roll up using the mat to help and press firmly at the top to seal (dampen edge if necessary to help seal). Repeat with remaining ingredients to form four rolls.
5. Using sharp wet knife, cut each roll into 6 to 8 pieces and arrange on serving platter. Serve soy sauce as a dipping sauce if you wish. If you are not serving right away, wrap rolls with plastic wrap or cover with a damp tea towel.

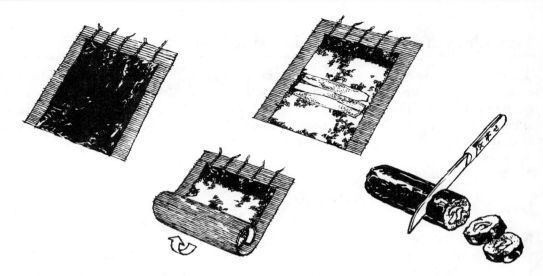

Cheddar Cheese Coins

These cheese coins make a delicious snack on their own, or they can be served with soup or dips.

Makes 6 dozen

2 cups	grated aged Cheddar cheese (about 8 oz/ 250 g)	500 mL
1/2 cup	unsalted butter	125 mL

1 cup	all-purpose flour	250 mL
1 tsp	dry mustard	5 mL
1 tsp	Worcestershire sauce	5 mL
1/4 tsp	Tabasco sauce	1 mL

1. Combine cheese with butter until creamed. Beat in flour, mustard, Worcestershire sauce and Tabasco. Mix until dough is formed.
2. Shape into two logs (as you would do for refrigerator cookies) about 1 1/2 inches (4 cm) in diameter and about 10 inches (25 cm) long. Wrap in waxed paper and refrigerate for a few hours or overnight.
3. Slice rolls carefully into 1/4-inch (5 mm) slices and place on buttered baking sheets (or line baking sheets with parchment paper). Bake in a preheated 375°F (190°C) oven for 7 to 9 minutes, or until just beginning to turn golden. Cool on wire racks.

Muffulata and Mortadella in Mini Pitas

The muffulata is a New Orleans specialty. It actually refers to a flat bun that is often used to make huge, luscious cold-cut sandwiches. The olive salad can also be used as part of an antipasta platter, or it can be pureed into a delicious spread for crackers. You can make the sandwiches with the salad alone or use cheese instead of the mortadella or ham.

Makes 24 mini pitas

1 cup	green olives stuffed with pimentos	250 mL
1/2 cup	pitted black olives (preferably Kalamata)	125 mL
1	4-oz (110 g) jar marinated artichokes, drained	1
1 tbsp	finely chopped hot pickled peppers	15 mL
1/2 tsp	dried oregano	2 mL
1/2 tsp	freshly ground black pepper	2 mL
2	cloves garlic, minced	2
2 tbsp	extra-virgin olive oil	25 mL
24	mini pitas	24
12	very thin slices mortadella or ham, halved	12
2 tbsp	chopped fresh parsley	25 mL

1. Chop olives coarsely with artichokes. Combine in bowl with pickled peppers, oregano, pepper, garlic and olive oil. (If you prefer, the olives can be semi or completely pureed.)
2. Cut the top 1/2 inch (1 cm) off the pitas and open the pockets. Fold the mortadella halves and stick into the pitas so that the top of the mortadella sticks out. Stuff some of the olive salad inside. Sprinkle with parsley. Arrange pitas upright in a basket lined with a pretty napkin.

Crabcakes with Chili Mayonnaise

The chili mayonnaise also makes a great dipping sauce for Cajun Style Shrimp "Popcorn" *(page 53)* or any other fried appetizer. If you wish, you can start with commercial mayonnaise and add the remaining ingredients, beginning with the red pepper. These can also be served as a first course.

Makes 16 to 20 small crabcakes

CHILI MAYONNAISE

2	egg yolks	2
2 tbsp	Dijon mustard	25 mL
2 tbsp	red wine vinegar or lemon juice	25 mL
1/2 tsp	salt	2 mL
1/2 tsp	freshly ground black pepper	2 mL
3/4 cup	vegetable oil	175 mL
3/4 cup	extra-virgin olive oil	175 mL
1	sweet red pepper, roasted, peeled, seeded and pureed	1
1/2 tsp	Tabasco sauce	2 mL
1/2 tsp	cayenne pepper	2 mL
1/2 tsp	chili powder	2 mL
1 tbsp	dry mustard	15 mL

CRABCAKES

3 tbsp	mayonnaise	50 mL
2	eggs	2
1 tbsp	Dijon mustard	15 mL
1 tsp	dry mustard	5 mL
1/4 tsp	Tabasco sauce	1 mL
1/4 tsp	cayenne pepper	1 mL
1/2 tsp	salt	2 mL
1/4 tsp	freshly ground black pepper	1 mL
1 lb	cooked crabmeat, defrosted	500 g
2 tbsp	chopped pimento	25 mL
1/3 cup	cooked or frozen corn niblets	75 mL
1 tbsp	chopped fresh parsley	15 mL
1 cup	fresh breadcrumbs	250 mL
1/3 cup	vegetable oil (approx.)	75 mL

1. To make mayonnaise, combine egg yolks, Dijon mustard, vinegar, salt and pepper in large stainless-steel or glass bowl.
2. Combine the oils in large measuring cup. Start adding the oil slowly to the egg-yolk mixture, beating with a whisk. When you have added about 1/2 cup (125 mL) oil, add it more quickly until all the oil has been absorbed. For a thinner mayonnaise, do not use as much oil. (If you are using a food processor, combine yolks with mustard, vinegar, salt, pepper and 1/4 cup/50 mL oil in work bowl fitted with metal blade. With machine running, slowly drizzle in remaining oil.)
3. Add red pepper, Tabasco, cayenne, chili powder and dry mustard. Taste and adjust seasoning if necessary. Reserve.
4. To make crabcakes, in large bowl, combine 3 tbsp (50 mL) mayonnaise, eggs, mustards, Tabasco, cayenne, salt and pepper.
5. Squeeze excess moisture from crab with your hands. Pick over carefully to remove bits of shell and cartilage. Add crab, pimento, corn, parsley and bread-crumbs to egg mixture. Stir together.
6. Shape mixture into 16 to 20 patties.
7. In skillet, heat oil on medium-high heat. Cook patties for about 3 minutes per side, or until nicely browned and cooked through. Drain on paper towels. Serve with chili mayonnaise.

A Lighter Side: Instead of using mayonnaise as a base for the chili mayonnaise, use low-fat sour cream or low-fat unflavored yogurt. Cook crabcakes in a non-stick pan lightly brushed with oil, or steam or bake them.

Barbecued Steak in Flour Tortillas

Although you could serve this as a main course, I like it better as an appetizer at informal barbecues.

Makes approximately 20 rolls

3 tbsp	extra-virgin olive oil	50 mL
1 tsp	freshly ground black pepper	5 mL
1/4 tsp	dried rosemary	1 mL
2 lb	sirloin steak (1 1/2 inches/4 cm thick)	1 kg
3 tbsp	red wine vinegar	50 mL
1 tbsp	Dijon mustard	15 mL
1	clove garlic, minced	1
1/3 cup	chopped fresh parsley	75 mL
1/3 cup	chopped fresh basil	75 mL
1/3 cup	chopped fresh watercress	75 mL
1/2 cup	extra-virgin olive oil	125 mL
	Salt and freshly ground black pepper to taste	
3	tomatoes, halved, seeded and diced	3
20	6-inch (15 cm) flour tortillas, or 10 pita breads cut in half	20
8	leaves Boston or Romaine lettuce	8

1. Combine olive oil with pepper and rosemary. Brush on steak.
2. Heat barbecue or broiler and brush grill or broiler pan with oil. Grill steak for 7 to 8 minutes per side for rare. Cool for at least 10 minutes and carve into thin slices on the diagonal.
3. In bowl, combine vinegar with mustard and garlic. Stir in herbs and watercress. Whisk in olive oil. Taste and add salt and pepper. Add tomatoes, toss and allow to marinate until ready to prepare sandwiches.
4. Wrap tortillas or pita bread in foil and warm in a preheated 350°F (180°C) oven for 5 minutes, or grill on barbecue for 20 to 30 seconds per side.
5. Arrange beef, tomato salad, lettuce and tortillas separately on the buffet table. To make a roll, place meat in the center of the tortilla and top with some salad and lettuce. Fold up bottom edge and roll tortilla up tightly. Eat carefully.

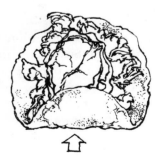  

Salad Sticks

These are so refreshing and clean-tasting! You can close them up completely or leave them open at one end. You can use cooked chicken or fish instead of the shrimp. The dressing can also be used as a dipping sauce.

Makes 12 to 16 rolls

PEANUT DRESSING

1 tsp	peanut butter	5 mL
1/4 tsp	hot red chili flakes	1 mL
1/2 tsp	oriental sesame oil	2 mL
1 tbsp	rice wine or mirin	15 mL
2 tbsp	orange juice	25 mL
3 tbsp	soy sauce	50 mL

SALAD STICKS

3 oz	thin rice vermicelli noodles	100 g
16	8-inch (20 cm) rice paper wrappers	16

8	Romaine lettuce leaves, shredded	8
1	large carrot, cooked and grated	1
16	shrimp, cooked and cut in half lengthwise	16
3 tbsp	chopped fresh coriander	50 mL
3 tbsp	chopped fresh chives or green onions	50 mL

1. To make dressing, blend peanut butter with chili flakes, sesame oil, rice wine and orange juice. Stir in soy sauce. Reserve.
2. To cook rice vermicelli, soak noodles in cold water for 5 minutes. Cook in boiling water for 5 minutes. Rinse and drain well and reserve.
3. To soften rice paper wrappers, dip one at a time into warm water for about 20 seconds. Lay out in a single layer on a clean damp tea towel (I usually work with four wrappers at a time).
4. In the center of each wrapper, arrange a little lettuce, grated carrot and some noodles. Place two shrimp halves vertically down the center of each. Sprinkle with coriander and chives. Spoon 1 tsp (5 mL) dressing over each.
5. Fold up bottom edge (and fold down top edge if you want them completely enclosed) and roll tightly starting at one side. If not serving right away, arrange on a damp tea towel and cover with second damp towel. Store in the refrigerator.

RICE PAPER WRAPPERS   *Rice paper wrappers are very versatile and a nice change from spring roll wrappers. They are also useful for people who are allergic to wheat (be sure to check the label first, to make sure the rice flour has not been blended with wheat flour). They can be fried, deep-fried, steamed, baked or used raw.*

Before using the wrappers, dip them into warm water for 10 seconds. Then place them on damp tea towels in a single layer. (I usually work with four wrappers at one time.)

Middle Eastern Eggplant Salad in Mini Pitas

I like to use the microwave to cook eggplant *(see below)* as it greatly reduces the cooking time. It turns this dish into something you can cook on the spur of the moment instead of having to plan it well ahead of time. You can serve this inside mini pitas, or you can make pita chips *(page 18)* and use this as a dip (place some finely chopped tomato and parsley in the center to add color).

Makes 48 appetizers

1	eggplant (1 lb/500 g)	1	1/2 tsp	dried oregano	2 mL	
2	cloves garlic, finely chopped	2	1/4 tsp	freshly ground black pepper	1 mL	
2 tbsp	lemon juice	25 mL	1/4 tsp	Tabasco sauce	1 mL	
2 tbsp	extra-virgin olive oil	25 mL	1 tbsp	chopped fresh coriander or parsley	15 mL	
1 tsp	oriental sesame oil	5 mL	24	mini whole wheat pitas	24	

1. Prick eggplant a few times with a fork and place on baking sheet. Bake in a preheated 425°F (220°C) oven for 45 to 50 minutes, or until tender. Cool, peel and cut into chunks.
2. Place eggplant with remaining ingredients except pitas in work bowl of food processor fitted with metal blade. Chop finely or puree until smooth. Adjust seasoning to taste.
3. Cut mini pitas in half. Open slightly. Fill with a little of the salad. Arrange slightly upright so that the filling does not fall out.

MICROWAVING EGGPLANT   *To microwave eggplant for spreads or dips, place the eggplant in a microwave-safe dish and pierce the skin in a few places. Microwave on High (100%) for 7 to 10 minutes, or until the eggplant is tender. When the eggplant is cool, peel and chop or puree.*

Thai Crabcakes with Peanut Coriander Pesto

This is a wonderfully delicious version of the more traditional crabcake. Instead of binding it with breadcrumbs, I've used ground scallops, which give the crabcakes a very different texture. The flavor of the coriander and ginger is also quite different and unusual. You can also serve these as a sit-down first course.

Makes 16 to 20 small crabcakes

PEANUT CORIANDER PESTO

1/4 cup	peanut butter	50 mL
2 tbsp	soy sauce	25 mL
1 tsp	oriental sesame oil	5 mL
1/2 tsp	oriental chili paste	2 mL
2 tbsp	lemon or lime juice	25 mL
1/2 cup	mayonnaise, sour cream or unflavored yogurt	125 mL
2 tbsp	chopped fresh chives	25 mL
1/4 cup	chopped fresh coriander	50 mL

CRABCAKES

2 tbsp	vegetable oil	25 mL
4	green onions, chopped	4
3	cloves garlic, finely chopped	3
1 tbsp	chopped fresh ginger root	15 mL
1 tbsp	grated lemon peel	15 mL
1/4 tsp	hot red chili flakes	1 mL
1	egg	1
1 tbsp	Dijon mustard	15 mL
1/2 tsp	Tabasco sauce	2 mL
1/2 tsp	salt	2 mL
1/4 tsp	freshly ground black pepper	1 mL
1 tsp	oriental sesame oil	5 mL
8 oz	fresh scallops	250 g
1 lb	cooked crabmeat (squeeze out excess liquid)	500 g
1/2 cup	fresh breadcrumbs *(page 25)*	125 mL
1/2 cup	chopped fresh coriander	125 mL
1/3 cup	vegetable oil	75 mL

1. In bowl, blend all ingredients for Peanut Coriander Pesto. Reserve.
2. Heat 2 tbsp (25 mL) oil in a skillet on medium-high heat. Cook green onions, garlic, ginger, lemon peel and chili flakes until fragrant and tender.
3. In separate bowl, combine egg with mustard, Tabasco, salt, pepper and sesame oil. Stir in green onion mixture.
4. Puree scallops and combine with herb and egg mixture.
5. Squeeze crab dry again and stir into scallop mixture. Add breadcrumbs and coriander.
6. Shape mixture into 16 to 20 small patties. (If mixture is too moist and does not seem to be holding together, add more breadcrumbs.)
7. Heat 1/3 cup (75 mL) oil in large skillet on medium-high heat. Cook patties for about 3 minutes on each side, or until nicely browned and cooked through. Drain on paper towels. Serve with pesto.

A Lighter Side: Instead of the pesto, use Peanut Dressing (page 45). Fry patties in a non-stick pan lightly brushed with oil, or steam or bake them.

Vietnamese Spring Rolls

These can be made a few hours ahead and deep-fried at the last minute, or they can be fried and then reheated briefly in a 400°F (200°C) oven.

Lettie Lastima, who works at the cooking school, is from the Philippines, and recommends soaking rice noodles in cold water before cooking. They always turn out great.

Makes 30 small or 16 large rolls

8 oz	boneless skinless chicken breasts	250 g	1 tbsp	finely chopped fresh ginger root	15 mL
2 tbsp	soy sauce	25 mL	2	cloves garlic, finely chopped	2
1 tbsp	hoisin sauce	15 mL	3	green onions, finely chopped	3
1 tbsp	water	15 mL	1	sweet red pepper, seeded and cut into thin julienne	1
2 tsp	frozen orange juice concentrate	10 mL	3 tbsp	chopped fresh coriander	50 mL
1 tsp	peanut butter	5 mL	30	triangular sheets of rice paper wrappers, or 16 rounds	30
1/2 tsp	oriental chili paste	2 mL	6 cups	vegetable oil	1.5 L
1/4 tsp	oriental sesame oil	1 mL			
2 tsp	cornstarch	10 mL			
8	dried shiitake mushrooms	8			
2 oz	thin rice vermicelli noodles	60 g			
2 tbsp	vegetable oil	25 mL			

1. Cut chicken into thin strips about 1 1/2 inches (4 cm) long.
2. In large bowl, combine soy sauce, hoisin, water, juice, peanut butter, chili paste and sesame oil until smooth. Stir in cornstarch. Add chicken and stir to coat well. Allow to marinate for at least 15 minutes.
3. Cover mushrooms with warm water and allow to soak for 15 to 30 minutes, or until softened. Drain well and rinse. Discard stems and slice caps into thin strips.
4. Meanwhile, break noodles into 1 1/2-inch (4 cm) pieces and cover with cold water. Allow to soak for 5 minutes. Cook in boiling water for 5 minutes. Drain. Rinse with cold water. Drain well.
5. Heat 2 tbsp (25 mL) oil in wok or skillet. Add ginger, garlic and green onions. Cook for 30 seconds. Add pepper strips and mushrooms. Cook for 3 minutes. Add chicken with juices and cook for 3 to 4 minutes, or just until chicken is cooked through. Stir in noodles and coriander. Cool.
6. Dip wrappers one at a time into warm water and lay out on damp tea towel in a single layer. (Wrappers should soften quickly.) Place a spoonful of filling in the center of each wrapper (I usually work with four wrappers at a time). Fold up bottom flap, fold down top flap and roll up to enclose filling.
7. Heat 6 cups (1.5 L) oil to medium-high heat in wok or Dutch oven. Cook rolls a few at a time (they tend

to stick together) for about 5 minutes, turning to brown all sides. Drain on rack. Serve plain or with Peanut Dressing *(page 45)*.

A Lighter Side: These can be steamed for 15 minutes instead of deep-fried. They can also be baked at 400°F (200°C) for 20 to 25 minutes, until brown. Or they can be eaten "uncooked."

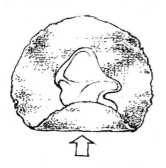 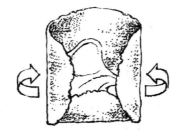 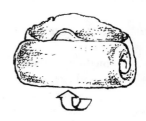

Tomato and Cheese Quesadillas

I make these in my spa cooking classes, and no one can believe that they are low in calories. That's perfect low-fat food!

Makes 8 quesadillas (24 appetizers)

2	chipotle or jalapeño chilies	2
1 cup	diced mild green chilies	250 mL
3	tomatoes, seeded and diced	3
1	clove garlic, minced	1
1/4 cup	chopped fresh coriander	50 mL

8	10-inch (25 cm) flour tortillas (white or whole wheat)	8
2 cups	grated low-fat mozzarella cheese (about 8 oz/250 g)	500 mL

1. Puree chipotle peppers with green chilies. Reserve.
2. In bowl, combine diced tomatoes with garlic and coriander.
3. Spread about 1 tbsp (15 mL) chili paste over one half of each tortilla. (This is hot, so only use the quantity you wish — freeze any paste that you do not use.) Spoon one-eighth of the tomato mixture over the chili paste. Sprinkle each with about 2 tbsp (25 mL) cheese. Fold the plain half over the cheese and press gently.

4. Place tortillas on baking sheet lined with parchment paper.
5. Just before serving, bake in a preheated 400°F (200°C) oven for 12 to 15 minutes, until cheese is melted and tortilla browns lightly.
6. Allow to rest for 3 minutes. Cut each tortilla into thirds. Serve as is or with low-fat yogurt mixed with chopped coriander and green onions for dipping.

Shrimp Packages with Coriander

These elegant little packages are different and exciting. Although it is much easier to buy the shrimp already cleaned, if you do them yourself, try to leave the tails on to act as natural handles for eating the shrimp! (Lots of people eat that piece as well, by the way.)

Makes approximately 24 packages

1 lb	medium shrimp, shelled and cleaned	500 g
2	cloves garlic, minced	2
2 tbsp	chopped fresh ginger root	25 mL
1/4 tsp	hot red chili flakes	1 mL
1/2 tsp	oriental sesame oil	2 mL
1 cup	chopped fresh coriander	250 mL
1/3 cup	chopped fresh chives or green onions	75 mL
1/2 tsp	salt	2 mL
1/2 tsp	freshly ground black pepper	2 mL
24	8-inch (20 cm) rice paper wrappers	24
2 tbsp	vegetable oil	25 mL

1. Pat shrimp dry.
2. For herb mixture, combine garlic with ginger, chili flakes, sesame oil, coriander, chives, salt and pepper.
3. Soak rice paper wrappers one at a time in warm water for about 20 seconds. Arrange in a single layer on a clean, damp tea towel (I usually work with four at a time). Fold up the bottom sixth of each wrapper as shown. Place a shrimp in the middle of each, with the tail piece sticking out a bit. Place some herb mixture on top of shrimp. Fold the right, then the left side of the wrapper over the shrimp. Fold down the top quarter. Fold up the shrimp and then fold down the two sides. The shrimp should be enclosed completely, with the tail jutting out a bit.
4. Heat oil in a large skillet (or two skillets) on medium-high heat and cook wrappers in a single layer for about 2 minutes on each side, or just until shrimp is cooked through. Serve on their own or with Peanut Dressing *(page 45)*.

A Lighter Side: These can also be steamed for 10 to 15 minutes or baked on a well-oiled baking sheet at 375°F (190°C) for 25 minutes.

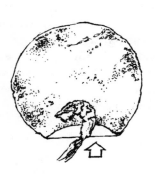
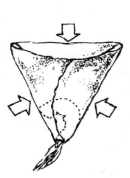

Shrimp Satays

Shrimp is an entertaining treat in most homes because of its cost. You can also prepare this with cubes of chicken breast or lamb leg. These kabobs can be served plain, as there is enough flavor in the marinade. (If you want to use the extra marinade for the dipping sauce, cook it for about 5 minutes after removing the uncooked shrimp.) Or, if you prefer, use Peanut Coriander Pesto *(page 47)* as a dipping sauce. Serve the satays hot or at room temperature.

Makes approximately 24 kabobs

2	cloves garlic, minced	2
1 tbsp	chopped fresh ginger root	15 mL
1/3 cup	coconut cream (tinned)	75 mL
2 tbsp	hoisin sauce	25 mL
2 tbsp	peanut butter	25 mL
2 tbsp	soy sauce	25 mL
1 tsp	oriental chili paste or Tabasco sauce	5 mL
1 tsp	oriental sesame oil	5 mL
2 lb	medium shrimp, shelled and cleaned	1 kg
1/4 cup	chopped fresh coriander or green onions	50 mL

1. In large bowl, combine garlic, ginger, coconut cream, hoisin sauce, peanut butter, soy sauce, chili paste and sesame oil. Blend until smooth.
2. Add shrimp to marinade and stir to coat well. Allow to marinate for 30 minutes at room temperature, or up to 2 hours in the refrigerator.
3. Have about 25 6-inch (15 cm) skewers ready. (Bamboo skewers should be soaked for a few hours in cold water before using.) Thread 2 shrimp on each skewer.
4. Heat barbecue or broiler and brush grill or broiler pan with oil. Arrange skewers on grill or hot broiler pan. Cook for about 3 minutes per side. Sprinkle with fresh coriander or green onions.

Crispy Wings with Coriander Dip

There are so many chicken wing recipes that it is hard for me to choose a favorite, but this is one of them. Although the breading mixture sounds spicy, it really isn't. And for those who like more heat, there's the dip! The breading mixture also works well for fish and shrimp. And the dip is good with corn chips.

Makes approximately 40 pieces

3 lb	chicken wings (about 20)	1.5 kg
1 cup	all-purpose flour	250 mL
1 cup	yellow cornmeal	250 mL
2 tbsp	ground cumin	25 mL
2 tsp	salt	10 mL
2 tsp	freshly ground black pepper	10 mL
2 tsp	cayenne pepper (or less to taste)	10 mL
3	eggs	3

CORIANDER DIP

1 1/2 cups	sour cream	375 mL
1/2 cup	mayonnaise	125 mL
2 cups	chopped fresh coriander	500 mL
1/2 cup	chopped fresh chives or green onions	125 mL
4	jalapeño chilies, seeded and minced	4
1 tsp	salt	5 mL

1. Discard wing tips or save for stock *(page 98)*. Separate each wing into two parts. Pat dry with paper towels.
2. In flat dish, combine flour with cornmeal, cumin, salt, pepper and cayenne. Beat eggs in another flat dish. Dip wings first into flour mixture, shaking off any excess. Dip wings next into egg mixture, allowing excess to drain off. Redip wings into flour mixture, pressing mixture in firmly. Place on rack to dry slightly if not cooking immediately.
3. Oil baking sheet lightly. Place wings on baking sheet. Bake in a preheated 375°F (190°C) oven for 20 minutes. Turn wings and bake for 30 to 35 minutes longer, until crisp and brown.
4. For dip, in bowl, combine sour cream with mayonnaise. Stir in coriander, chives, chilies and salt. (If dip is not hot enough for you, add Tabasco sauce to taste.)
5. Serve wings with dip on large platter. (Remember to have a bowl handy for the bones, and lots of napkins.)

A Lighter Side: Use 2 cups (500 mL) low-fat sour cream instead of sour cream and mayonnaise in dip.

Cajun Style Shrimp "Popcorn"

Anything deep-fried does taste better cooked at the last minute. But this dish can be made ahead and reheated in a 450°F (230°C) oven for 5 minutes. If you use small shrimp or cut the larger ones into pieces, they will resemble popcorn (and you will eat them almost as quickly!). Serve this with Chili Mayonnaise *(page 43)*.

Serves 8 to 10

1 cup	all-purpose flour	250 mL		1/2 tsp	cayenne pepper	2 mL
2 tbsp	yellow cornmeal	25 mL		1 cup	beer	250 mL
1 tsp	salt	5 mL		1/2 tsp	Tabasco sauce	2 mL
1/2 tsp	freshly ground black pepper	2 mL		1 1/2 lb	shrimp, shelled and cleaned	750 g
1/2 tsp	freshly ground white pepper	2 mL			Vegetable oil for frying	

1. In large bowl, combine flour with cornmeal and spices.
2. Stir beer into flour mixture and blend only until ingredients are well combined. Stir in Tabasco.
3. Pat shrimp dry. Add shrimp to batter and stir well to coat. (Or, add shrimp to batter one at a time just before frying.)
4. Heat 2 inches (5 cm) oil in large deep pan to approximately 400°F (200°C).

Carefully add shrimp one by one to the hot oil. You may have to cook them in two or three batches, depending on the width of your pan. Cook each batch for approximately 2 minutes on each side.
5. Drain on wire racks set above a baking pan. Serve immediately.

SHELLING AND CLEANING SHRIMP   *Although there are many gadgets that you can buy to shell and clean shrimp, the best tools are your hands and a sharp knife. Break the shell apart from underneath and wiggle off the tail rather than breaking it off. That way you will save the delicate piece of shrimp lodged at the end. "Deveining" really means removing the intestinal tract. To do this, run your sharp knife along the upper middle length of the shrimp — about 1/4 inch (5 mm) deep. With the tip of your knife, pull out the black "vein" running lengthwise. (This is usually done for aesthetic purposes and is often ignored with smaller shrimp.) Rinse the shrimp if they seem especially dirty.*

Many fish stores sell cleaned shrimp, though they may be slightly more expensive.

Spicy Cajun Popcorn

This is a great appetizer to serve when you are in a hurry. It is so easy to prepare but really perks up the appetite because of the spices.

Makes approximately 12 cups (3 L)

3 tbsp	vegetable oil	50 mL
2/3 cup	popping corn	150 mL
1/3 cup	unsalted butter	75 mL
1	clove garlic, minced	1
1 tsp	Tabasco sauce (or less to taste)	5 mL
1/2 tsp	cayenne pepper	2 mL
1/2 tsp	salt (or more to taste)	2 mL
1/4 tsp	freshly ground black pepper	1 mL
1/4 tsp	freshly ground white pepper	1 mL

1. To pop corn, heat oil in Dutch oven on medium-high heat. Add corn. Cover and shake until popping begins. Lift lid slightly to allow steam to escape, continuing to shake pan over heat. When popping stops, transfer to large bowl. (Popcorn can also be popped using your favorite method.)

2. In small saucepan, melt butter over low heat and add garlic. Stir in Tabasco, cayenne, salt, black and white peppers.

3. Toss with popcorn. Serve immediately.

A Lighter Side: Pop corn in hot-air popper and toss with last four ingredients only.

FIVE SPICE DIPPING SAUCE *Serve this with Vietnamese Spring Rolls (page 48) or Shrimp Packages with Coriander (page 50). Five spice powder sometimes contains more than five spices. You can buy it in oriental food stores or specialty stores, or you can make your own in a blender or spice grinder by grinding together equal amounts of star anise, fennel seed, cinnamon, cloves and Sichuan peppercorns.*

To make the dipping sauce, combine 2 tbsp (25 mL) soy sauce, 2 tbsp (25 mL) Worcestershire sauce or black Chinese vinegar, 2 tbsp (25 mL) HP steak sauce and 1/4 tsp (1 mL) five spice powder. Taste and adjust seasoning if necessary. Makes about 1/3 cup (75 mL).

Swordfish Teriyaki

You can make this glaze in larger batches and keep it refrigerated until ready to use, but be sure to use only as much as you need at a time, or you will get raw fish or meat juices in the marinade you wish to save.

Serves 12

1/2 cup	soy sauce	125 mL
1/2 cup	rice wine or mirin	125 mL
1/2 cup	granulated sugar	125 mL
1	clove garlic, smashed	1
1	1-inch (2.5 cm) piece fresh ginger root, smashed	1
3	slices lemon peel	3
	Stems of fresh coriander (handful)	
1 1/2 lb	swordfish, sliced 1/4 inch (5 mm) thick	750 g
3 tbsp	chopped fresh coriander	50 mL

1. Combine soy sauce, rice wine, sugar, garlic, ginger, lemon peel and coriander stems in medium saucepan and bring to a boil. Reduce heat slightly and cook until mixture is reduced by about half and is thick and syrupy. Cool.
2. Cut fish into long 1 1/2-inch (4 cm) strips. Pat fish dry.
3. Weave swordfish onto 12 skewers, piercing fish in three or four spots to secure it.
4. Heat barbecue or broiler and brush grill or broiler pan with oil. Cook fish for 1 minute and turn. Brush with glaze. Cook fish for 2 minutes and turn. Brush with glaze. Cook fish for 1 minute. Brush and turn once more. (Fish should be cooked through but still moist and juicy after 4 or 5 minutes of cooking.) Serve with fresh coriander on top.

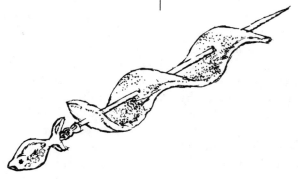

BAMBOO SKEWERS *If you are cooking with wooden skewers, be sure to soak them for a few hours in cold water first, to prevent them from burning on the barbecue or in the oven.*

Ricotta Pastries

A few years ago when I was visiting friends Loni Kuhn and Jana Allen in San Francisco, they set up a whirlwind restaurant tour for me. For every meal we went somewhere different with about eight people so we could try nearly everything on the menu. Take a bite and pass it on were the key words for six days. The last evening, Jana had us all over for dinner. Dinner was wonderful and these were the appetizers. But it actually would not have mattered what she served, as long as everyone ate the same thing and we didn't have to take a bite and pass it on.

Makes approximately 48 pastries

1 cup	all-purpose flour	250 mL
1/4 tsp	salt	1 mL
1/2 cup	unsalted butter, cold, diced	125 mL
1/2 cup	ricotta cheese	125 mL
2 tbsp	Dijon mustard	25 mL
3 tbsp	chopped fresh rosemary	50 mL
20	2-inch (5 cm) fresh basil leaves	20
10	fresh sage leaves, cut in half lengthwise	10
10	anchovies, cut in half lengthwise	10
1	egg	1
1/2 tsp	salt	2 mL
2 tbsp	sesame seeds	25 mL
3 tbsp	freshly grated Parmesan cheese (preferably Parmigiano Reggiano)	50 mL

1. In food processor fitted with the metal blade, combine flour with 1/4 tsp (1 mL) salt. Add butter. Process until butter is in tiny bits. Add ricotta and process only until dough is moistened. Remove from work bowl and gather into ball by hand so as not to over-process. (Dough can also be mixed by hand.) Wrap dough and chill for 1 hour.
2. Roll dough out into a rectangle about 6 x 16 inches (15 x 40 cm). Cut in half lengthwise so there are two pieces 3 x 16 inches (7.5 x 40 cm).
3. Spread dough with mustard. Cut each piece into 3/4 x 3-inch (2 x 7.5 cm) strips. Sprinkle some strips with rosemary and line some with basil or sage leaves. Place an anchovy strip down others.
4. Line two baking sheets with parchment paper. Twist strips to enclose filling and arrange on prepared baking sheets.
5. In small bowl, beat egg with 1/2 tsp (2 mL) salt. Brush egg over tops of pastries. Sprinkle some with sesame seeds and some with cheese.
6. Bake in a preheated 350°F (180°C) oven for 20 to 25 minutes, or until lightly browned. Serve warm or at room temperature.

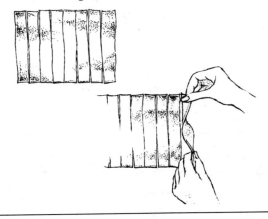

Marinated Spiced Olives

Not only is this great to serve as a little treat before dinner, but these olives are also a perfect hostess gift. Store them in the refrigerator but serve at room temperature. This recipe will fill four small jars.

Makes 2 cups (500 mL)

1 cup	black olives (preferably Kalamata)	250 mL
1 cup	green olives	250 mL
1/4 tsp	hot red chili flakes	1 mL
2 tbsp	whole black peppercorns	25 mL
2 tbsp	whole white peppercorns	25 mL
1/2 tsp	dried thyme	2 mL
1/2 tsp	dried oregano	2 mL
4	cloves garlic, peeled but whole	4
	Peel of 1 lemon, cut into strips	
1 cup	extra-virgin olive oil (approx.)	250 mL

1. In bowl, combine all ingredients except olive oil. Place in jar and cover with olive oil. Seal jar and marinate at room temperature for 2 weeks. Every day or two turn jar to ensure even spicing.

2. If you are giving this away as gifts, bottle in smaller jars. After 2 weeks store in the refrigerator. Olive oil will turn slightly opaque and thicken, but will return to normal consistency at room temperature.

GARLIC   *Garlic is essential to good-tasting food. I never worry about how much to use when the garlic is going to be cooked, because cooking makes it soft and sweet-tasting. But I am cautious when using it raw, as it is much more potent. In salad dressings, dips and spreads where raw garlic is called for, I mince it or use a garlic press so that no one gets a piece of it! But in cooking, I always chop it, as the juices released in pulverized garlic may burn or stick when added to hot oil.*

To peel garlic, place a clove on the counter and slam it gently with the side of your knife. The peel will slip off.

Garlic powder and garlic salt are dreadful and bitter-tasting; they are no substitute for fresh garlic. The minced garlic sold in oil is also inferior. Compare these products to fresh garlic, and you will easily taste and smell the difference.

If you love the flavor of garlic in dips and salad dressings but find raw garlic too strong, use the trick I learned from Santa Fe chef and restauranteur Mark Miller. Place the unpeeled cloves in a heavy skillet and cook over low heat, shaking the pan often, for 40 to 45 minutes, or until the garlic is slightly browned on the outside and cooked on the inside. Peel before using. The garlic will have a wonderful smoky, earthy flavor.

Eggplant Sandwiches

Anyone who thinks they don't like eggplant will change their minds when they taste these.

Makes approximately 36 pieces

2	long thin eggplants (about 2 x 8 inches/ 5 x 20 cm) Salt	2
4 oz	mortadella, ham or salami thinly sliced	125 g
6 oz	provolone, fontina or mozzarella cheese, thinly sliced	175 g

1 cup	all-purpose flour	250 mL
4	eggs, lightly beaten	4
2 1/2 cups	fresh breadcrumbs *(page 25)*	625 mL
1/2 cup	freshly grated Parmesan cheese (preferably Parmigiano Reggiano)	125 mL
1/4 cup	chopped fresh parsley	50 mL
2 tbsp	extra-virgin olive oil	25 mL

1. Slice each eggplant crosswise into 1/4-inch (5 mm) slices. You should have about 36 slices. Place in colander and sprinkle with salt. Place colander in sink or large bowl and allow to rest for 30 minutes. Drain eggplant well, rinse and pat dry.
2. Cut slices of meat and provolone to fit eggplant. Make sandwiches with one layer of meat and cheese only. Press the sandwiches together firmly.
3. Place flour in one shallow dish and eggs in a second dish. Combine breadcrumbs, Parmesan cheese and parsley in another. Dredge eggplant with flour first; dust off any excess. Dip into egg and then press into crumbs. Repeat until all sandwiches are breaded.
4. Arrange sandwiches in a single layer on baking sheets lined with parchment paper. Drizzle with olive oil.
5. Bake in a preheated 375°F (190°C) oven for 20 minutes. Turn sandwiches and continue to bake for 20 minutes.
6. To serve, cut into halves.

A Lighter Side: Use low-fat cheese inside the sandwiches. Omit the meat and the olive oil.

PARCHMENT PAPER   *Parchment paper is a non-stick baking paper that you can use to line baking sheets and loaf pans to prevent food from sticking.*

Onion Pakoras

These are wonderfully tasty fritters. They can be deep-fried or shallow-fried as described below. If you cook them ahead, arrange them in a single layer on a baking sheet and reheat in a preheated 425°F (220°C) oven for 5 to 7 minutes. The chickpea flour is available at health food stores and any East Indian grocery.

Makes approximately 18

1 cup	besan (chickpea flour)	250 mL
2 tsp	ground cumin	10 mL
1 tsp	salt	5 mL
3/4 tsp	cayenne pepper	4 mL
1/2 tsp	baking soda	2 mL
1/4 cup	chopped fresh coriander	50 mL
2/3 cup	ice water	150 mL
1	potato (about 8 oz/250 g), cleaned and cut into tiny julienne sticks	1

2	red onions, thinly sliced	2
1 cup	vegetable oil	250 mL

DIPPING SAUCE

2 tbsp	oriental chili paste	25 mL
2 tsp	rice vinegar	10 mL

1. In bowl, combine chickpea flour with cumin, salt, cayenne, baking soda and fresh coriander. Stir in ice water.
2. Stir in potatoes and onions.
3. Heat oil in a deep skillet on medium-high heat. Drop batter by the spoon-ful into the hot oil and flatten slightly like a pancake. Cook for 2 to 3 minutes per side until well browned and cooked through. Drain well.
4. For the dipping sauce, combine chili paste with vinegar. Use dip sparingly.

Shrimp Spring Rolls with Mustard Lime Dipping Sauce

Spring roll wrappers filled with all sorts of oriental and non-oriental ingredients are a delicious treat.

Makes 20 to 24 spring rolls

FILLING

12 oz	cooked shrimp	375 g
2 tbsp	extra-virgin olive oil	25 mL
1	red onion, slivered	1
2	cloves garlic, finely chopped	2
1/4 tsp	hot red chili flakes	1 mL
8 oz	fresh shiitake or oyster mushrooms, sliced	250 g
10	sun-dried tomatoes, slivered	10
3 tbsp	chopped fresh basil or coriander	50 mL

	Salt and freshly ground black pepper to taste	
24	spring roll wrappers	24
1	egg	1
2 tbsp	all-purpose flour	25 mL
1 tbsp	water	15 mL
6 cups	vegetable oil	1.5 L

MUSTARD LIME DIPPING SAUCE

2 tbsp	soy sauce	25 mL
2 tbsp	lime juice	25 mL
1 tbsp	Dijon mustard	15 mL
1/4 tsp	oriental sesame oil	1 mL

1. Dice shrimp and reserve.
2. Heat olive oil in large skillet on medium-high heat. Add onion, garlic and chili flakes. Cook until tender and wilted but do not brown. Add mushrooms and cook for a few minutes. Add shrimp and sun-dried tomatoes. Cook for 2 minutes. Add basil and salt and pepper to taste. Cool.
3. Separate spring rolls wrappers and arrange on counter. For the "glue," in small bowl, combine egg, flour and water. Place a spoonful of filling on each wrapper. Fold up bottom over the filling. Fold in the sides. Spread a little egg mixture on the unfolded edge and roll up wrapper. Press to secure.
4. Just before serving, heat vegetable oil in a wok or Dutch oven. Oil should be at approximately 375°F (190°C). Cook spring rolls for about 3 minutes on each side until nicely browned.
5. Drain on paper towels. These can be made ahead and reheated at 400°F (200°C) for about 20 minutes.
6. For dipping sauce, combine ingredients together and pour into attractive bowl.

A Lighter Side: Place the spring rolls on a parchment paper-lined baking sheet instead of deep-frying. Brush them with vegetable oil and bake in preheated 400°F (200°C) oven for 20 to 25 minutes, until browned and crisp.

Santa Fe Pizza

I often tell students that when they are having trouble finding ingredients, if they have a neighborhood restaurant that specializes in the type of food they are looking for, sometimes the chef or manager will sell some. So one Sunday I was testing recipes and discovered I was out of tortillas. I called the Mexican restaurant across the street and asked if they had any extra flour tortillas they could sell me. They checked and said they were almost all out but could spare four. I thought it was strange for a Mexican restaurant to be down to their last four flour tortillas, but I thought it was lovely that they would share them with me. So I said I'd be right there. On my way over I planned how to halve my recipe, etc. When I got to the restaurant, they gave me four packages of one hundred each! So if you are buying from restaurants, be very specific.

When I make these I usually bake two, serve them and bake the second batch while eating the first so they are always fresh. You can assemble them about one hour in advance.

Makes 32 wedges

CHILI PASTE

3/4 cup	chopped mild green chilies	175 mL
2	chipotle chilies, chopped *(page 36)*	2
2 tbsp	adobo sauce (from chipotles)	25 mL
1 tbsp	extra-virgin olive oil	15 mL

TOMATO SALSA

5	tomatoes, seeded and finely chopped	5
2	cloves garlic, minced	2
1/2 cup	chopped fresh coriander	125 mL
	Salt and freshly ground black pepper to taste	
2 cups	grated Monterey Jack cheese (about 8 oz/250 g)	500 mL
2 cups	grated mild Cheddar cheese (about 8 oz/250 g)	500 mL
4	9-inch (23 cm) flour tortillas	4
1/4 cup	chopped fresh coriander	50 mL

1. Puree mild green chilies with chipotles, adobo sauce and oil. Reserve.
2. In bowl, combine tomatoes, garlic, 1/2 cup (125 mL) coriander and salt and pepper. Place in strainer and allow to drain until ready to use.
3. In separate bowl, combine grated cheeses.
4. Place 2 tortillas on a baking sheet in a single layer. (Usually you can fit two on one sheet even if they overlap slightly.) Bake in a preheated 400°F (200°C) oven for 2 to 3 minutes. Turn tortillas over.
5. Spread each tortilla with chili paste. It is hot, so use your own judgment as to how much to put on. Any extra can be frozen. (It is also delicious in grilled cheese sandwiches.) Sprinkle with tomato mixture and then with cheese. Top with a little more coriander.
6. Just before serving, bake pizzas for 10 to 12 minutes, until cheese is melted and bubbling. Let rest for 5 minutes before cutting into wedges to serve.

Barbecued Pizza with Peppers and Chèvre

When we first tested our barbecued pizza, we didn't know what to expect. Would it burn? Would it drip through the grates? Would we eat it so fast we could hardly breathe? No, no, yes.

Use this technique of grilling the dough first and then topping the pizza with whatever you like. The Grilled Eggplant, Red Pepper and Red Onion Salad *(page 146)* would be very good on this dough with or without a sprinkling of cheese. The topping from the Santa Fe Pizza *(page 61)* would also be terrific. Or to the topping in this recipe you could add chopped garlic and/or hot red chili flakes.

If you are making the dough in a food processor, use 3/4 cup (175 mL) room temperature water rather than warm. Combine the dry ingredients in the work bowl fitted with the metal blade. With the machine running, add the yeast/water mixture and process until the dough forms a ball, cleaning the sides of the bowl. Then proceed with the recipe.

If you do not have a barbecue or grill, simply sear the dough in a very hot heavy skillet before adding the toppings and baking. You can also barbecue the crust ahead of time and then bake just before serving.

Although this dough is extremely easy to make, and nothing you buy could be quite as good, you can use 1 1/4 lb (625 g) frozen pizza or bread dough instead.

Makes 6 individual pizzas, 36 hors d'oeuvre

CRUST

1 tbsp	granulated sugar	15 mL
1 cup	warm water	250 mL
1	envelope dry yeast (1 tbsp/15 mL)	1
2 cups	all-purpose flour	500 mL
1/4 cup	yellow cornmeal	50 mL
1 tsp	salt	5 mL
2 tbsp	extra-virgin olive oil	25 mL

TOPPING

1/4 cup	extra-virgin olive oil	50 mL
1/2 tsp	salt	2 mL
1 tbsp	chopped fresh rosemary	15 mL
6 oz	chèvre (creamy mild goat cheese), crumbled	175 g
2	sweet red peppers, roasted, seeded and cut into strips	2
2	tomatoes, seeded and chopped	2
1/4 cup	chopped fresh basil	50 mL
1/2 cup	freshly grated Parmesan cheese (preferably Parmigiano Reggiano)	125 mL

1. For crust, dissolve sugar in 1/4 cup (50 mL) very warm water in 2-cup (500 mL) measure. Sprinkle yeast over water and allow to rest for 10 minutes, or until mixture has doubled in volume.

2. Meanwhile, in large bowl, combine flour with cornmeal and salt.

3. When yeast has bubbled up, stir mixture down and combine with remaining 3/4 cup (175 mL) warm water and 2 tbsp (25 mL) olive oil. Add this to

flour mixture and knead to form ball of dough. Add more flour if dough is too sticky. Dough should be very moist, but it should not stick to your fingers. Knead dough for about 10 minutes. (If using mixer with dough hook, knead for 5 minutes; if using food processor, mix for 1 minute.)

4. Place dough in bowl brushed with olive oil. Turn dough until it is coated with oil on all sides. Cover with plastic wrap and allow dough to rise in warm place—about 45 minutes.
5. Punch dough down and divide into six pieces. Roll or flatten each piece to form 6-inch (15 cm) circle. Brush one side with olive oil and place oiled side down on a preheated barbecue or grill. Brush top with olive oil. Grill for 1 minute. Turn. Brush top with a little more oil, dust with salt and rosemary. Grill for 1 minute and place on a baking sheet. Grill remaining pizzas.
6. Sprinkle each pizza with crumbled chèvre, red peppers, tomatoes, basil and Parmesan.
7. Bake in a preheated 400°F (200°C) oven for 15 minutes. Serve one pizza to each guest or cut each into four to six pieces for hors d'oeuvre.

ROSEMARY PEPPER FOCCACIA   *Make a different kind of pizza by brushing the barbecued pizza dough with olive oil. Then sprinkle it with coarse grindings of black pepper, some sea salt and about 1 tbsp (15 mL) chopped fresh rosemary. Bake for 15 minutes at 400°F (200°C).*

BARBECUED PIZZA SALAD   *One of my students, Audrey MacLean, owns a restaurant in Guelph, Ontario, called Doug's Place. She gave me the delicious idea of brushing pizza dough with olive oil and salt before baking or barbecuing, then topping the crust with a salad. This way, one very large crouton is on the bottom! It makes a great light lunch.*

YEAST   *You can buy dry yeast or cake (moist) yeast. Cake yeast should be used immediately or frozen. One cube is equivalent to one envelope or 1 tbsp (15 mL) dry yeast. I usually use the regular dry yeast, but you can also buy instant dissolving yeast that can be mixed in with the flour without being dissolved first (follow the package directions). Any kind of yeast will be "killed" if the liquid you use is too hot; the yeast action will be slower if the liquid is too cold.*

Wild Mushroom and Artichoke Frittata

Instead of serving these as is, you can cut them even smaller and fit them into mini pita breads for a picnic-style appetizer.

Makes approximately 24 squares

1 oz	dried wild mushrooms	30 g
1 cup	warm water	250 mL
2 tbsp	unsalted butter or olive oil	25 mL
2	cloves garlic, finely chopped	2
pinch	hot red chili flakes	pinch
5	eggs	5
1/4 cup	warm water	50 mL
1 cup	grated fontina cheese (about 4 oz/125 g)	250 mL
1/2 cup	freshly grated Parmesan cheese (preferably Parmigiano Reggiano)	125 mL
1/2 cup	fresh breadcrumbs (page 25)	125 mL
1/4 tsp	salt	1 mL
1/4 tsp	freshly ground black pepper	1 mL
2 tbsp	chopped fresh basil or parsley	25 mL
2	4-oz (125 mL) jars marinated artichokes, chopped with oil	2
1/4 cup	chopped sun-dried tomatoes	50 mL

1. Place dried mushrooms in bowl and cover with warm water. Allow to soak for 20 minutes. Drain, saving both the mushrooms and the liquid. Rinse mushrooms and chop finely. Strain liquid through paper towel-lined sieve.
2. Heat butter or oil in skillet on medium-high heat. Cook garlic and chili flakes until tender and fragrant. Add mushrooms and liquid and cook until liquid reduces by half.
3. In large bowl, beat eggs together. Stir in water, cheeses, breadcrumbs, seasonings, artichokes, sun-dried tomatoes and mushroom mixture.
4. Transfer to a buttered 8-inch (2 L) square baking dish and bake in a preheated 350°F (180°C) oven for 30 to 35 minutes. Allow to rest for 15 minutes before cutting into squares.

A Lighter Side: Omit the fontina cheese and use half the Parmesan. Use 1 tbsp (15 mL) olive oil instead of the butter.

WILD MUSHROOMS   *Fresh wild mushrooms are becoming increasingly available. If you are used to using dried porcini mushrooms, remember that the fresh ones will not have as intense a flavor (I often combine the two).*

Soak dried mushrooms in warm water for about 20 minutes, until softened. Strain the liquid through a sieve lined with paper towels. Rinse the mushrooms well, as there can be a lot of sand and grit in them. If the recipe does not use the soaking liquid, be sure to freeze it for sauces, soups, etc., as it has a marvelous flavor.

There are many varieties of fresh wild mushrooms — oyster, shiitake, morels, chanterelles, cèpes, etc., but you are usually lucky to find two or three varieties at any one time. I remove the stems if they are hard (use them in stocks), slice the caps and saute them gently in butter and olive oil with lots of garlic, pepper and parsley.

Spinach Turnovers

This pastry is delightful to work with and can be used for any savory turnover or dough. If you have a garden full of Swiss chard, use it in place of the spinach.

Makes approximately 36 turnovers

PASTRY

1 cup	unsalted butter, cold, diced	250 mL
2 cups	all-purpose flour	500 mL
8 oz	cream cheese, cold, diced	250 g

FILLING

1/4 cup	raisins	50 mL
1 1/2 lb	fresh spinach	750 g
2 tbsp	extra-virgin olive oil	25 mL
2	cloves garlic, finely chopped	2
4	anchovies, finely chopped	4
2 oz	ham, finely chopped	60 g
1/4 cup	chopped toasted pine nuts or almonds	50 mL
1/4 tsp	freshly ground black pepper	1 mL
	Salt to taste	
1	egg, lightly beaten	1

1. For pastry, cut butter into flour until it is in tiny bits. Cut in cream cheese until dough comes together into a ball. Divide dough into two pieces, wrap in plastic wrap and refrigerate until ready to use.
2. For filling, soak raisins in boiling water for 15 minutes. Drain well. Reserve.
3. Wash spinach thoroughly and remove tough stems. Cook until wilted. Drain well and squeeze out most of the water. Chop.
4. Heat olive oil in large skillet on medium-high heat. Add garlic and cook until fragrant but do not brown. Add anchovies and ham and cook together until anchovies "melt" into mixture. Add spinach and cook until any liquid evaporates. Add raisins, pine nuts and pepper and combine well. Taste and add salt only if necessary.
5. Roll out balls of dough and cut out 3- or 4-inch (7.5 or 10 cm) circles. Reroll extra dough and cut out more circles — you should have at least 36. Place a little filling on one side of each circle. Brush edges with beaten egg and fold over. Place on baking sheet. Brush turnovers with egg and refrigerate until ready to bake.
6. Bake in a preheated 375°F (190°C) oven for 20 to 30 minutes, or until nicely browned.

A Lighter Side: Use low-fat pressed cottage cheese instead of the cream cheese in the pastry.

REROLLING PASTRY   *When rerolling scraps of dough to make more turnovers, pastry or cookies, do not knead the pieces into a ball again. Simply press the scraps together gently and then reroll to avoid overhandling the dough as much as possible.*

Spicy Glazed Almonds

This is the kind of thing you just can't stop eating. If it is too spicy, cut down on the cayenne and Tabasco. This recipe also works well with pecans. The nuts can be frozen and make great hostess gifts or take-home presents.

Makes approximately 3 cups (750 mL)

1/4 cup	corn syrup	50 mL	1 tsp	Tabasco sauce	5 mL
2 tbsp	unsalted butter	25 mL	1/2 tsp	cayenne pepper	2 mL
2 tbsp	water	25 mL	1/2 tsp	freshly ground white or	2 mL
1 tsp	salt	5 mL		black pepper	
2 tsp	paprika	10 mL	1 lb	whole almonds with skins	500 g

1. Place corn syrup, butter and water in saucepan and bring to a boil. Stir in spices.
2. Add almonds and stir well to coat.
3. Spread almonds on baking sheet lined with parchment paper. Bake in a preheated 275°F (120°C) oven for 1 hour. Stir every 15 minutes to separate almonds.

Red Pepper Bruschetta

When I roast peppers *(page 106)* I like to do lots and freeze the extra so that I can make this appetizer any time. You can use Swiss cheese instead of fontina.

Makes 16 pieces

8	slices crusty French or Italian bread, 3/4 inch (2 cm) thick and 4 inches (10 cm) wide	8
1/4 cup	extra-virgin olive oil	50 mL
1	clove garlic, cut in half	1
8	thin slices fontina cheese, cut to fit bread (about 4 oz/125 g)	8

3	sweet red peppers, roasted, peeled and diced	3
	Salt and freshly ground black pepper to taste	
1/4 cup	chopped fresh basil or parsley	50 mL

1. Arrange slices of bread on baking sheet in a single layer. Broil or grill until lightly browned — watch carefully. Turn and toast the other side. (Centers should remain soft.)
2. Brush one side of bread lightly with oil and rub with garlic. Top each slice of bread with a slice of cheese.
3. Meanwhile, in bowl, combine remaining oil with red peppers. Season to taste with salt and pepper. Stir in basil.
4. Spread this mixture evenly over bread slices.
5. Just before serving, bake in a preheated 400°F (200°C) oven for 5 to 10 minutes, until thoroughly heated and cheese melts. Cut each slice in half.

A Lighter Side: Omit the olive oil; use low-fat mozzarella cheese instead of fontina.

Tomato Bruschetta

This is a fresh-tasting appetizer that can be made on the spur of the moment.

Makes approximately 10 pieces

2	cloves garlic, minced	2
4	tomatoes, seeded and diced	4
2 tbsp	chopped fresh basil or parsley	25 mL
	Salt and freshly ground black pepper to taste	

1	12-inch (30 cm) French stick	1
1/4 cup	extra-virgin olive oil	50 mL
1/3 cup	freshly grated Parmesan cheese (preferably Parmigiano Reggiano)	75 mL

1. In bowl, combine garlic with tomatoes, basil, salt and pepper.
2. Cut bread diagonally into slices 3/4 inch (2 cm) thick. Arrange in single layer on baking sheet. Brush with oil. Broil for 1 to 2 minutes, or until crisp and browned. Reduce oven to 425°F (220°C).
3. Turn slices over. Spoon tomato mixture over bread. Sprinkle with Parmesan. Bake for 8 to 10 minutes, or until heated through.

A Lighter Side: Omit the olive oil.

Scallion Pancakes

This is a very easy way to make delicious Hunan pancakes. They are great as an appetizer or served alongside a main course.

Serves 6 to 8

8	flour tortillas	8
3 tbsp	oriental sesame oil	50 mL
1	egg, beaten	1
1/2 cup	chopped green onions	125 mL
1/4 tsp	salt	1 mL
1/2 tsp	freshly ground black pepper	2 mL
2 to		500 to
3 cups	vegetable oil	750 mL

1. Arrange 4 tortillas on the counter. Brush them with sesame oil. Brush with egg and sprinkle with green onions, salt and pepper.
2. Cover each tortilla with a second one and press together firmly.
3. Heat 1-inch (2.5 cm) vegetable oil in a deep skillet large enough to hold a tortilla. Cook tortillas one at a time until golden-brown on each side. Drain well and cut into quarters.

Crostini with Chèvre and Black Olives

Crostini can be made with bread toasted in the following manner and any kind of topping spread over it. This combination is particularly flavorful. You can use 1/3 cup (75 mL) olive paste instead of the olives. (Stir it in after creaming the cheese so the spread does not become completely purple.) Or you can omit the olives completely.

Serves 8

8	slices crusty French or Italian bread, about 1/2 inch (1 cm) thick and 4 inches (10 cm) wide	8	1/2 cup	black olives (preferably Kalamata), pitted and diced	125 mL
2 tbsp	extra-virgin olive oil	25 mL	1/4 tsp	freshly ground black pepper	1 mL
12 oz	chèvre (creamy mild goat cheese), crumbled	375 g	1/4 cup	chopped fresh herbs (parsley, basil, thyme, rosemary, etc.)	50 mL
1	clove garlic, minced	1			

1. Arrange slices of bread on baking sheet in a single layer. Broil or grill until lightly browned—watch carefully. Turn and toast other side lightly (centers should remain soft). Brush bread lightly with oil.
2. In bowl, combine chèvre with garlic, olives, pepper and herbs.
3. Spread cheese mixture on bread toasts.
4. Serve crostini as is or, just before serving, run bread under a preheated broiler for about 2 minutes, or just to warm cheese. Or, bake in a preheated 400°F (200°C) oven for 3 to 5 minutes. Watch carefully. Serve immediately.

A Lighter Side: Omit the olive oil on the bread. Instead of the chèvre, use half chèvre and half low-fat pressed cottage cheese.

CLARIFIED BUTTER *Clarified butter is usually used when you want the taste of butter but, because you are cooking on direct heat, don't want the butter to burn. It can be used for cooking crêpes, omelets or in other recipes where butter tends to burn easily.*

To make it, melt 2 cups (500 mL) butter and place in a 2-cup (500 mL) glass measure. Refrigerate. When the butter becomes solid again, the milky liquid will accumulate at the bottom and the hard clarified "butter fat" will be on top. The milky residue is the part that burns and causes crêpes and eggs to stick to the pan. Use it in soups or breads or discard it. Clarified butter will keep for months, and although it isn't essential to refrigerate it, I do.

Beggar's Purses

Filled with sour cream and caviar, these sweet little pouches are a treat to eat. They can also be filled with diced smoked salmon instead of caviar.

Makes 12 to 16

CREPES

4	eggs	4
1 cup	all-purpose flour	250 mL
1/2 cup	milk	125 mL
1/2 cup	water	125 mL
1 tbsp	granulated sugar	15 mL
1/2 tsp	salt	2 mL
3 tbsp	unsalted butter, melted	50 mL

1. In bowl, beat eggs with flour, milk, water, sugar, salt and melted butter. Cover bowl and allow batter to rest at room temperature for 1 hour (or longer in refrigerator).
2. To prepare crepes, brush an 8-inch (20 cm) non-stick crêpe or omelet pan with a little unsalted butter and heat. Add a ladleful of batter, swirl around to coat the bottom of pan and then pour remaining batter in pan back into bowl of batter. This will result in a smooth thin crêpe. Cook crêpe until nicely browned, flip and cook second side for about 30 seconds. (The second side is never as attractive as the first and should be used on the inside.) As crêpes are ready, stack on plate. You should be able to get 12 to 16 crêpes from this batter.

FILLING

8 oz	cream cheese	250 g
3 tbsp	sour cream	50 mL
2 oz	salmon caviar	60 g

RIBBONS

20	green onions	20

3. Beat cheese and sour cream until smooth.
4. Cut white portion off green onions and use for another recipe. Blanch the green parts in boiling water for 30 seconds. Refresh under cold water and pat dry. These strips will be used to tie the "purses."
5. Arrange crêpes on counter with "second" side facing up. Place a spoonful of sour cream mixture on each. Top with a little caviar. Wrap the crêpe around the filling like a little sac and tie with a green onion ribbon.

A Lighter Side: Use low-fat pressed cottage cheese instead of the cream cheese and low-fat unflavored yogurt instead of the sour cream. When making the crêpes, use all water instead of the milk, and reduce the butter by half.

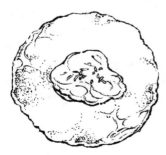  

Pizza Pie Pie

This is a "pie," not just a pizza. It has a top and bottom crust. It's easy to make, fun to layer and great to serve in 2-inch (5 cm) squares for a party. It is also perfect for picnics and tastes great cold.

Instead of this pastry, you can make your own favorite pastry (make enough for a double-crust pie) or use traditional pizza dough. You can also use commercial pastry or bread dough, or phyllo pastry.

Makes one 15 x 10-inch (45 x 25 cm) pie

PASTRY

4 cups	all-purpose flour	1 L
2 tsp	salt	10 mL
1 1/4 cups	unsalted butter, diced	300 mL
3	eggs	3
1/4 cup	extra-virgin olive oil	50 mL
1/2 cup	ice water (approx.)	125 mL

FILLING

4 oz	pepper salami, thinly sliced	125 g
2 cups	grated mozzarella cheese (about 8 oz/250 g)	500 mL
4 oz	ham or other salami, thinly sliced	125 g
1 cup	tomato sauce or tomato puree	250 mL
8 oz	mortadella, thinly sliced	250 g
1 cup	freshly grated Parmesan cheese (preferably Parmigiano Reggiano)	250 mL
1/2 tsp	freshly ground black pepper	2 mL
1/4 cup	chopped fresh basil or parsley	50 mL
4	eggs, lightly beaten	4
1/4 cup	extra-virgin olive oil	50 mL

1. For pastry, combine flour with salt in large bowl. Cut in butter until it is in tiny bits.
2. In separate bowl, combine eggs with oil and 1/3 cup (75 mL) ice water. Drizzle over the flour and gather together into a ball. If pastry seems dry, add remaining water. Divide dough in half.
3. Roll out one half of dough to fit 15 x 10-inch (37 x 25 cm) jellyroll pan (with a 1-inch/2.5 cm lip). Fit dough into pan.
4. Arrange salami over the bottom crust. Sprinkle grated mozzarella cheese over the salami. Top with slices of ham. Spread with tomato sauce. Arrange mortadella over tomato sauce. Sprinkle with grated Parmesan, pepper and basil. Drizzle eggs as evenly as possible over top. Drizzle most of olive oil over eggs but save a little to brush on top of finished pastry.
5. Roll out second ball of dough to fit on top. Crimp edges and prick top with a fork. Brush with remaining olive oil.
6. Bake in a preheated 375°F (190°C) oven for 45 to 55 minutes, until pastry is browned and crisp. Cool for 20 minutes before serving.

Quick Tomato Pizza

This pizza crust is a very easy and quick bread batter. It is flavored with rosemary and has a nice crunch from the cornmeal. Because the dough does not need to rise, assemble the ingredients for the topping before making the crust.

Makes 12 to 16 pieces

TOPPING

4	ripe tomatoes, cored and seeded	4
1/2 cup	chopped fresh basil or parsley	125 mL
2	cloves garlic, minced	2
1 tsp	salt	5 mL
1/4 tsp	freshly ground black pepper	1 mL
pinch	hot red chili flakes	pinch
2 cups	grated mozzarella cheese (about 8 oz/250 g)	500 mL
1/2 cup	pitted black olives (preferably Kalamata), halved	125 mL
1	4-oz (110 g) jar marinated artichokes, drained and halved	1
1/2 cup	freshly grated Parmesan cheese (preferably Parmigiano Reggiano)	125 mL

CRUST

2 cups	all-purpose flour	500 mL
1 cup	whole wheat flour	250 mL
1/2 cup	yellow cornmeal	125 mL
1 tbsp	chopped fresh rosemary (or 1/2 tsp/2 mL dried)	15 mL
1 tbsp	granulated sugar	15 mL
1 tsp	salt	5 mL
2 tsp	baking powder	10 mL
1 tsp	baking soda	5 mL
1 2/3 cups	unflavored yogurt	400 mL
1/3 cup	extra-virgin olive oil	75 mL

1. Chop tomatoes coarsely. Drain well. In bowl, combine tomatoes with basil, garlic, salt, pepper and chili flakes. Have remaining topping ingredients ready.
2. For dough, in large bowl, combine flours, cornmeal, rosemary, sugar, salt, baking powder and baking soda. Stir together well.
3. In separate bowl, combine yogurt with oil. Pour liquid ingredients over dry ingredients and knead together lightly into a ball. Brush a 15 x 10-inch (37 x 25 cm) jellyroll pan generously with olive oil. Press dough evenly into pan.
4. Sprinkle half the mozzarella cheese over the dough. Drain tomatoes again and spread over cheese. Arrange olives and artichokes over the tomatoes and sprinkle with remaining mozzarella and Parmesan.
5. Bake in a preheated 400°F (200°C) oven for 20 to 25 minutes, or until pizza is puffed and cheese is lightly browned. Cut in squares before serving.

Phyllo Pouches with Spinach and Feta Cheese

Phyllo pastry is very versatile and can be used as a wrapper for Asian-flavored fillings as well as European. In this recipe I have shaped the pastries into little pouches, but you can also make them into the more traditional triangles *(page 76)* or rolls. Lately, phyllo dough has been used instead of puff pastry in many desserts.

These pastries can also be frozen *(page 76)*.

Makes approximately 60 pieces

3 tbsp	unsalted butter or extra-virgin olive oil	50 mL	2	eggs, lightly beaten	2
1	small onion, diced	1	2 tbsp	chopped fresh dill	25 mL
1	clove garlic, finely chopped	1	1/4 tsp	grated nutmeg Salt and freshly ground black pepper to taste	1 mL
1 lb	fresh spinach, well cleaned, dried and chopped into small pieces	500 g	1/2 cup	fine dry breadcrumbs	125 mL
			1 lb	phyllo pastry	500 g
8 oz	feta cheese, crumbled	250 g	3/4 cup	unsalted butter, melted (approx.)	175 mL

1. For filling, heat butter or oil in large deep skillet on medium-high heat. Cook onions and garlic until sweet and tender, but do not brown. Add spinach and cook, stirring, until it wilts.

2. Transfer spinach mixture to bowl and cool slightly. Stir in crumbled cheese, eggs, seasonings and breadcrumbs. Reserve.

3. To make pouches, unwrap dough and cover with damp tea towel. Have melted butter and a pastry brush beside work surface. Have two baking sheets close by.

4. Remove four sheets of dough at a time. Keep the rest covered. Sheets should be about 16 x 12 inches (40 x 30 cm). Arrange one sheet on work surface and brush with butter. Top with another, brush and repeat until you have four layers. Cut layers into six equal "squares." (If you would like this to look a little fancier, cut phyllo into squares before brushing with butter. Layer sheets of pastry as shown in illustration.) Place a teaspoon of filling in the center of each square and gather pastry together to form a pouch, twisting dough around the top of the filling. Place on baking sheet. Repeat until all the filling is used.

5. Bake pouches in a preheated 400°F (200°C) oven for 20 to 25 minutes, or until nicely browned.

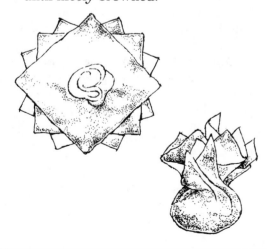

Fish Cakes Tempura

These fish cakes are somewhat sweet and have a lovely flavor and texture. They can be eaten as is or dipped into soy sauce or a mixture of one part five-spice powder and four parts salt. I like these cold.

Makes 15 3-inch (7.5 cm) patties

1 lb	white-fleshed fish fillets (perch, whitefish, Boston bluefish, cod, haddock, snapper, etc.)	500 g
1	egg	1
2 tbsp	rice wine or mirin	25 mL
2 tbsp	sushi vinegar	25 mL
2 tbsp	granulated sugar	25 mL
1/2 tsp	salt	2 mL
1/4 tsp	freshly ground black pepper	1 mL
1/2 cup	fresh white breadcrumbs *(page 25)*	125 mL
1	carrot, grated	1
1/2 cup	frozen peas, defrosted	125 mL
2	green onions, chopped	2

BATTER

1	egg	1
1/2 cup	ice water	125 mL
2/3 cup	all-purpose flour	150 mL
1/2 tsp	baking powder	2 mL
1/4 tsp	salt	1 mL
	Vegetable oil for frying	

1. Cut fish into 1-inch (2.5 cm) pieces and pat dry. Place in food processor fitted with metal blade and process with egg, rice wine, sushi vinegar, sugar, salt, pepper and breadcrumbs to form a dough-like mixture.
2. Stir in carrots, peas and green onions.
3. Shape fish into 15 thin patties, 1/2 inch (1 cm) thick and 3 inches (7.5 cm) in diameter (or make tiny patties). Refrigerate.
4. Prepare batter by beating egg with ice water in bowl.
5. In separate bowl, mix or sift flour with baking powder and salt. Stir into egg mixture. Place batter in shallow dish.
6. Heat 1/4-inch (5 mm) oil in large skillet on medium-high heat. Dip patties lightly into batter, allowing excess to run off. Cook for 2 to 3 minutes per side. Drain well. Serve warm or cold.

A Lighter Side: Omit the batter. Cook the patties in a small amount of vegetable oil, in a non-stick skillet.

Phyllo Triangles with Chèvre and Pesto

You can shape these into triangles or little pouches like the feta and spinach pastries *(page 74)*.

To freeze these, place the unbaked pastries on a baking sheet lined with plastic wrap. When frozen, pack into plastic bags. Before serving, arrange frozen pastries on a baking sheet and bake.

Makes approximately 60 pieces

1 lb	chèvre (creamy mild goat cheese)	500 g
1	recipe Pesto *(page 27)*	1
1 lb	phyllo pastry	500 g
3/4 cup	unsalted butter, melted (approx.)	175 mL
1/2 cup	fine dry breadcrumbs	125 mL
3 tbsp	sesame seeds	50 mL

1. Crumble cheese and toss with pesto sauce in bowl.
2. To make triangles, unwrap dough and cover with damp tea towel. Have melted butter and pastry brush beside work surface. Have two baking sheets close by.
3. Work with one piece of pastry at a time. Cut dough in half lengthwise. Brush one half with butter, sprinkle lightly with breadcrumbs and fold over lengthwise, making one long strip. Place a spoonful of filling in the bottom right corner. Brush rest of strip with butter, sprinkle with breadcrumbs and fold dough and filling up into a trianglar shape. Continue as shown, as if you were folding a flag. Brush with butter and sprinkle with breadcrumbs at all folds.
4. Arrange triangles on baking sheet and brush with butter. Sprinkle with sesame seeds and bake in a preheated 400°F (200°C) oven for 20 to 25 minutes, until nicely browned.

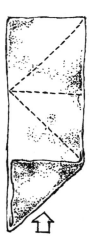

Crab Quesadillas with Coriander Salsa

Anytime you want to impress anyone, make these quesadillas. They can be made ahead and reheated in a 400°F (200°C) oven before serving. You can use cooked lobster or shrimp instead of the crab or, if you are allergic to shellfish, omit the seafood completely.

Makes approximately 30 pieces

1	7-oz (200 g) package frozen snow crab, defrosted	1
2 tbsp	mayonnaise	25 mL
1 1/2 cups	grated Monterey Jack cheese (about 6 oz/175 g)	375 mL
2 oz	chèvre (creamy mild goat cheese), crumbled	60 g
1/4 cup	diced mild green chilies	50 mL
2 tbsp	chopped fresh coriander	25 mL

10	9-inch (23 cm) flour tortillas	10
1	egg white, slightly beaten	1
	Vegetable oil for frying	

CORIANDER SALSA

1/2 cup	chopped fresh coriander	125 mL
1 cup	sour cream	250 mL
1 tbsp	lime juice	15 mL
1/4 tsp	Tabasco sauce	1 mL

1. Squeeze excess liquid from crab. Place in bowl. Stir in mayonnaise, Monterey Jack, chèvre, chilies and coriander. Taste and adjust seasoning if necessary.
2. Arrange 5 tortillas on counter. Spread crab filling over each tortilla, leaving a border of about 1/2 inch (1 cm). Brush border with egg white to help sticking. Place another tortilla on top of the filling and pinch edges together gently but firmly.
3. Heat about 1-inch (2.5 cm) oil in skillet (one that is larger than the tortillas!). Cook tortillas one at a time for about 3 minutes per side, until browned. Serve tortillas as they cook or place on a baking sheet and keep warm in a 200°F (100°C) oven.
4. To make salsa, combine coriander with sour cream, lime juice and Tabasco. Cut each quesadilla into six wedges and serve with salsa as a dip.

A Lighter Side: Use low-fat mozzarella instead of Monterey Jack. Instead of frying quesadillas, place on baking sheets and bake in a preheated 400°F (200°C) oven for 15 minutes. Or cook in a non-stick pan lightly brushed with clarified butter or olive oil.

Polenta Squares

Polenta, made by cooking cornmeal into a creamy mass, can be served in two ways. One style is soft and creamy *(see page 134 for a version with wild mushrooms)*. Or it can be made ahead and cooled in a baking pan or loaf pan. When cold, the polenta is cut into squares or slices and either fried, broiled, grilled, baked or eaten as is. This way, it makes a great base for spreads or other appetizers. To this cooked polenta you can add 1 cup (250 mL) grilled, peeled and diced red peppers, or 1/2 cup (125 mL) pitted and diced olives or sun-dried tomatoes. Serve it hot or cold. You can also buy instant polenta, which is actually quite good.

Makes approximately 24 3-inch (7.5 cm) squares

8 cups	water	2 L
1 tsp	salt	5 mL
1/4 tsp	freshly ground black pepper	1 mL
2 tbsp	extra-virgin olive oil	25 mL
2 cups	yellow cornmeal	500 mL

1. Bring water to a boil in large deep saucepan.
2. Add salt, pepper and olive oil.
3. Whisk in the cornmeal very, very slowly (using a whisk helps prevent the cornmeal from lumping). An Italian proverb says you should add the cornmeal so slowly that you can see each grain go in!
4. Switch to a long-handled wooden spoon and, stirring constantly to prevent sticking, cook polenta over medium heat for about 35 minutes. Be careful, as the mixture sometimes spits at you. (Some cooks even wear a long oven mitt.) Taste and adjust seasoning if necessary. Add grilled red peppers, diced sun-dried tomatoes, or diced and pitted black olives if you wish.
5. Pour mixture evenly into a 17 x 12-inch (45 x 30 cm) jellyroll pan lined with parchment paper. Cool before cutting into squares.

Microwave Instructions: Combine water with salt, pepper and cornmeal in a 12-cup (3 L) microwave-safe casserole. Stir. Cook on High (100%) for 12 minutes. Stir once or twice during cooking. Stir and allow to rest for 5 minutes. Pour into baking pan as above and cool.

4

First Courses

Scallops Provençale

Scallops are my favorite seafood. They are sweet, succulent and tender. I always try to buy fresh scallops, because their texture is usually far superior to the frozen. And for this recipe I like to use the larger sea scallops rather than the very small bay ones, for a silkier texture.

This can be served with lots of French bread, or it can be combined with fettuccine for a wonderful pasta dish. Use 1 lb (500 g) fettuccine.

Serves 8 to 10

6 tbsp	unsalted butter	90 mL
3	cloves garlic, finely chopped	3
1	shallot, finely chopped	1
3	tomatoes, peeled, seeded and finely chopped	3
1/3 cup	dry white wine	75 mL
1 1/2 lb	fresh scallops, cleaned	750 g
1/4 cup	chopped fresh parsley Salt and freshly ground black pepper to taste	50 mL

1. Melt 2 tbsp (25 mL) butter in large skillet on medium-high heat. Add garlic and shallots. Cook until very fragrant and tender but do not brown.
2. Add tomatoes and wine and cook until sauce is reduced and slightly thickened.
3. In second large skillet, melt 2 tbsp (25 mL) butter on medium-high heat. Add scallops in a single layer. Cover loosely with buttered parchment or waxed paper and cook for 3 to 4 minutes, or until they are just barely cooked. Add half the parsley, taste and season with lots of salt and freshly ground black pepper.
4. Using a slotted spoon, transfer scallops to tomato mixture. Reduce scallop cooking juices to 2 tbsp (25 mL) and stir in remaining 2 tbsp (25 mL) butter. Stir this mixture into scallops.
5. Serve scallops and sauce with remaining parsley sprinkled on top.

A Lighter Side: Use 2 tbsp (25 mL) olive oil for the sauce and another 2 tbsp (25 mL) olive oil to cook the scallops in place of the butter. Omit the final addition of butter.

Wild Mushroom Gratin

Fresh wild mushrooms are wonderful, but they can be really expensive. If you want to reduce the cost of this dish, use an additional pound of regular mushrooms instead of the fresh wild ones, but don't omit the dried mushrooms, as they add a very intense flavor.

Serve this with brioche toast *(page 93)* or toasted or grilled bread.

Serves 10

1 oz	dried wild mushrooms (cèpes or porcini)	30 g
1 cup	warm water	250 mL
2 tbsp	unsalted butter	25 mL
2	large shallots, diced	2
2	cloves garlic, finely chopped	2
1 lb	fresh button mushrooms, thickly sliced	500 g
1 lb	fresh wild mushrooms (combination of chanterelles, oyster, shiitake), tough stems removed, thickly sliced	500 g
1/4 cup	Cognac or brandy	50 mL
1/4 cup	dry Marsala or sherry	50 mL
3/4 cup	whipping cream	175 mL
1 tsp	salt	5 mL
1/2 tsp	freshly ground black pepper	2 mL

TOPPING

3/4 cup	fresh breadcrumbs *(page 25)*	175 mL
2 tbsp	chopped fresh parsley	25 mL
1 tbsp	chopped fresh basil	15 mL
1 tsp	chopped fresh thyme	5 mL
1/2 tsp	chopped fresh rosemary	2 mL
1/3 cup	freshly grated Parmesan cheese (preferably Parmigiano Reggiano)	75 mL
2 tbsp	unsalted butter, melted	25 mL

1. Soak dried mushrooms in warm water for 20 minutes. Strain liquid through paper towel-lined strainer and reserve. Rinse mushrooms and trim off any tough stems. Leave mushrooms as is or cut in half.
2. Heat butter in large skillet on medium heat. Add shallots and garlic and cook gently for 5 minutes, until very fragrant and tender. Add button mushrooms and cook for 5 minutes. Add soaked dried mushrooms and soaking liquid. Cook until almost all liquid has evaporated or been absorbed.
3. Stir in fresh wild mushrooms and combine well. Cook for 2 minutes. Add Cognac, Marsala and cream. Cook for 3 minutes.
4. With a slotted spoon, remove mushrooms to buttered 8-cup (2 L) gratin dish. Reduce sauce over high heat until thickened and spoon over mushrooms. Combine and season with salt and pepper.
5. In bowl, combine topping ingredients and sprinkle over mushrooms. Bake in a preheated 400°F (200°C) oven for 15 minutes, until browned.

A Lighter Side: Use 1/3 cup (75 mL) chicken stock instead of the whipping cream.

Thai Shrimp on Noodles

Sweetening foods with caramel is very typical of Thai cooking, and combined with the chilies creates a complex, wonderful blend. Thai fish sauce is used in Thai cooking as soy sauce is used in Chinese and Japanese cooking. It is available in most oriental markets.

Serves 8

1/4 cup	granulated sugar	50 mL
2 tbsp	water	25 mL
1/2 cup	boiling water	125 mL
1/4 cup	lemon juice	50 mL
2 tbsp	Thai fish sauce or soy sauce	25 mL
1/2 tsp	oriental chili paste (or more)	2 mL
2 tsp	cornstarch	10 mL
1 lb	broccoli, florets only	500 g

8 oz	thin rice vermicelli noodles	250 g
1/4 cup	vegetable oil	50 mL
2	cloves garlic, finely chopped	2
3	green onions, chopped	3
1 tsp	grated lemon peel	5 mL
1 1/2 lb	shrimp, shelled and cleaned	750 g
1/4 cup	chopped fresh coriander	50 mL
1/4 cup	pine nuts, toasted	50 mL

1. Prepare caramel by combining sugar with 2 tbsp (25 mL) water in small saucepan. Cook on medium-high heat, stirring until mixture is hot, and then stop stirring. With pastry brush dipped in cold water, brush sugar crystals on the inside of the pot down into the syrup. Cook until mixture turns golden-brown. Standing back, stir in boiling water. Cook for 30 to 60 seconds, or until smooth. Remove saucepan from heat and reserve.
2. In bowl, combine lemon juice, fish sauce, chili paste and cornstarch. Stir in caramel. Reserve.
3. In separate saucepan, cook broccoli florets in boiling water for 2 to 3 minutes, until bright-green. Drain and reserve.
4. Soak rice noodles in cold water for 5 minutes. Cook in pot of boiling water for 5 minutes. Drain well.
5. Heat oil in wok or skillet on medium-high heat. Add garlic, green onions and lemon peel and cook for 30 seconds, until very fragrant. Add shrimp and cook until barely pink. Add reserved sauce and combine well. Cook for 3 to 5 minutes, until shrimp are just cooked.
6. Place noodles on platter and top with shrimp mixture, coriander, broccoli and pine nuts.

RICE VERMICELLI NOODLES   *These very thin noodles (also called rice stick noodles) can be used in soups, fillings and as a base for stir-fried dishes. They should be soaked in cold water for 5 minutes before being boiled for 5 minutes. If they are deep-fried, deep-fry the noodles in very hot oil directly from the dried state, and watch them expand.*

Buckwheat Potato Blinis with Smoked Salmon

Blinis are usually yeast-risen buckwheat pancakes traditionally served with caviar. This is a faster no-yeast version that is great with caviar alone, or with the smoked salmon.

These blinis could also be made in 2-inch (5 cm) rounds for dainty little finger foods, as shown on the front cover.

Serves 8

BLINIS

1 1/4 lb	baking potatoes, peeled and cut up	625 g
3	eggs	3
1/2 cup	all-purpose flour	125 mL
1/3 cup	buckwheat flour	75 mL
1 tsp	salt	5 mL
1/2 tsp	freshly ground black pepper	2 mL
1/4 cup	unsalted butter, melted	50 mL
3/4 cup	light cream	175 mL

TOPPING

1 1/2 lb	smoked salmon, thinly sliced	750 g
1/2 cup	sour cream or crème fraîche (*page 11*)	125 mL
1/3 cup	chopped fresh chives	75 mL
2 tbsp	small capers (optional)	25 mL
2 oz	salmon caviar (optional)	60 g

1. For the blinis, cook potatoes in boiling salted water until tender. Drain well and mash. (You should have about 2 cups/500 mL.)
2. In large bowl, combine eggs with all-purpose flour, buckwheat flour, salt, pepper and melted butter. Stir in cream and cooled potatoes. Add more cream if necessary — batter should be the consistency of thin sour cream.
3. Brush an 8-inch (20 cm) non-stick skillet or omelet pan with butter and heat on medium-high. Add about 1/3 cup (75 mL) batter to skillet. Cook for a few minutes on each side until browned. Repeat with remaining batter. Keep blinis warm or reheat just before serving.

4. To serve, place one blini on each plate. Cover with a layer of smoked salmon. Drizzle sour cream or crème fraîche over the salmon. Sprinkle with chives and capers and/or caviar.

A Lighter Side: Use milk instead of cream in the batter. Use low-fat unflavored yogurt instead of sour cream or crème fraîche in the topping. Cook blinis in a non-stick pan without any butter.

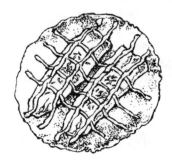

Baked Eggplant Parmesan

This is an irresistible appetizer. It can also be served as a side dish and is delicious cold on picnics. If you do not want to fry the eggplant, brush it with olive oil and broil or barbecue for a few minutes on each side until browned. The dish can be assembled ahead of time and baked just before serving.

Serves 8 to 10

3	large eggplants (3 lb/1.5 kg total)	3
1 tbsp	salt	15 mL
1/3 cup	vegetable oil	75 mL
1/3 cup	extra-virgin olive oil	75 mL
3	28-oz (796 mL) tins plum tomatoes, very well drained and chopped Freshly ground black pepper to taste	3
1 tbsp	chopped fresh oregano (or 1/2 tsp/2 mL dried)	15 mL
1/4 cup	chopped fresh basil or parsley	50 mL
4 cups	grated mozzarella cheese (about 1 lb/500 g)	1 L
1/2 cup	freshly grated Parmesan cheese (preferably Parmigiano Reggiano)	125 mL

1. Peel eggplants or leave peel on, as you wish. Slice into 1/4-inch (5 mm) slices. Sprinkle each slice with salt and place in a colander. Allow to drain for about 30 minutes. Pat eggplant dry.
2. Combine oils in one or two large deep skillets. Heat oil on medium-high heat and cook eggplant slices in batches until browned on both sides. (Use more oil if necessary.) Drain on racks or paper towels.
3. Place layer of eggplant slices in bottom of a 13 x 9-inch (3.5 L) casserole dish. Spread with some tomatoes.

Sprinkle with pepper, oregano and basil. Top with some grated mozzarella cheese. Repeat layers until everything is used, ending with a layer of cheese. Sprinkle top with Parmesan.

4. Bake in a preheated 400°F (200°C) oven for 30 minutes, or until mixture is golden and bubbling. Allow to rest for 10 minutes before serving. Serve hot, cold or at room temperature.

A Lighter Side: Brush the eggplant slices with olive oil and broil or grill instead of frying them. Use half the cheese.

Porcini Mushroom Quiche

The wonderful woodsy flavor of wild porcini mushrooms permeates this rich quiche.

Serves 8 to 10

PASTRY

1 1/2 cups	all-purpose flour	375 mL
1/4 tsp	salt	1 mL
1/4 cup	freshly grated Parmesan cheese (preferably Parmigiano Reggiano)	50 mL
1/2 cup	unsalted butter, cold, diced	125 mL
1/4 cup	ice water	50 mL

FILLING

1/2 oz	dried porcini mushrooms	15 g
1 cup	warm water	250 mL
2 tbsp	unsalted butter	25 mL
2	shallots, finely chopped	2
1 lb	fresh button mushrooms, sliced	500 g
3	eggs	3
2	egg yolks	2
1 1/2 cups	whipping cream or light cream	375 mL
1/2 cup	freshly grated Parmesan cheese (preferably Parmigiano Reggiano)	125 mL
1 tsp	salt	5 mL
1/4 tsp	freshly ground black pepper	1 mL
2 tbsp	chopped fresh parsley	25 mL

1. For pastry, combine flour, salt and cheese in large bowl. Cut in butter until it is in tiny bits. Sprinkle with ice water and gather dough together into a ball. Use a little more water only if necessary.
2. Roll dough out into a circle to fit a 10- or 11-inch (25 or 27.5 cm) quiche dish. Fit dough into pan. Trim edges. Line with parchment paper and fill with pie weights or raw rice or dried beans. Bake in a preheated 425°F (220°C) oven for 20 minutes. Remove weights and carefully remove paper. Cool slightly.
3. For filling, place dried mushrooms in bowl and cover with warm water. Allow to soften for 20 minutes. Strain soaking liquid through a paper towel-lined sieve. Reserve liquid. Rinse mushrooms thoroughly and chop.
4. Melt butter in large skillet on medium-high heat. Cook shallots until very fragrant, but do not brown. Add fresh mushrooms and chopped wild mushrooms and cook for a few minutes. Add reserved soaking liquid from wild mushrooms and cook until liquid evaporates or is absorbed by fresh mushrooms. Cool.
5. In large bowl, beat eggs, egg yolks and cream together. Beat in cheese, salt and pepper.
6. Spread mushrooms over bottom of crust. Pour cream/egg mixture over top and sprinkle with parsley. Bake in a preheated 350°F (180°C) oven for 40 to 45 minutes, or until top is slightly puffed and golden. Cool for 10 to 15 minutes before serving.

A Lighter Side: Roll pastry very thin. (Freeze extra pastry for another time.) Use another whole egg instead of the two yolks and use milk instead of cream in the filling.

Spa Pizza

Everyone loves pizza, but no one thinks of it as low-calorie fare. Enter the flour tortilla as the thin, crispy base with a topping of tomato salsa, and you can eat more than you thought possible. Change the toppings by adding small pieces of cooked or raw shrimp, rounds of olives, paper-thin slices of lean cooked sausage or anything else that strikes your fancy.

Serves 4 as a first course, or makes 32 individual wedges

4	8-inch (20 cm) flour tortillas	4

TOMATO SALSA

4	tomatoes, seeded and finely chopped	4
2	cloves garlic, minced	2
1/2 cup	chopped fresh basil	125 mL
1/4 cup	chopped fresh parsley	50 mL

2	green onions, chopped	2
2 tbsp	pine nuts, toasted	25 mL
1/2 tsp	hot red chili flakes	2 mL
1/2 tsp	freshly ground black pepper	2 mL
1/3 cup	freshly grated Parmesan cheese (preferably Parmigiano Reggiano)	75 mL

1. Place tortillas on baking sheets in a single layer. Bake in a preheated 400°F (200°C) oven for 5 minutes to crisp.
2. In bowl, combine tomatoes with garlic, basil, parsley, green onions, pine nuts, chili flakes and black pepper. Divide mixture among the four tortillas and spread evenly right to the edges. Sprinkle with cheese.
3. Just before serving, bake pizzas for 10 to 12 minutes, until sauce is bubbling and cheese is lightly browned. Serve whole or cut into wedges. (If serving in wedges, allow to cool for about 5 minutes before serving so that pizzas will be easier to handle.)

FOOD PROCESSOR PASTRY *To make pastry in the food processor, combine the dry ingredients in the work bowl fitted with the metal blade. Cut the cold butter, shortening or lard into chunks and add to the dry ingredients. Process with on/off pulses until the mixture is in small bits. Sprinkle the liquid over the flour mixture and process on/off until the flour is completely moistened and in pebble-like pieces. Remove the dough from the food processor and gather it into a ball with your hands.*

Red Onion and Mustard Tarts

This trick of lining the pastry shell with mustard is a "truc" I learned from Simone Beck when I took lessons with her fifteen years ago. The mustard adds a wonderful flavor but also protects the crust from becoming too moist from the filling.

These can also be baked in tiny muffin pans (you will get more tarts from the recipe).

Makes 24 2-inch (5 cm) tarts

PASTRY

1 1/2 cups	all-purpose flour	375 mL
1 tsp	dry mustard	5 mL
1/2 tsp	salt	2 mL
1/3 cup	unsalted butter, cold, diced	75 mL
1/3 cup	lard or shortening, cold, diced	75 mL
1/4 cup	ice water	50 mL
2 tbsp	Dijon mustard	25 mL

FILLING

2 tbsp	unsalted butter or vegetable oil	25 mL
1	red onion, thinly sliced	1
1	clove garlic, finely chopped	1
2	eggs	2
2/3 cup	light cream or whipping cream	150 mL
1/2 tsp	salt	2 mL
1/4 tsp	freshly ground black pepper	1 mL
1/4 tsp	Tabasco sauce	1 mL
pinch	grated nutmeg	pinch
2	green onions, finely chopped	2

1. In large bowl, combine flour, dry mustard and salt. Cut in butter and lard until you have tiny even-sized pieces. Sprinkle mixture with water and gather together quickly to form ball of dough. Add more water if necessary. Wrap in plastic wrap and refrigerate for 30 minutes before rolling.
2. Divide dough in half and roll out each half into a circle about 1/8 inch (3 mm) thick. Cut into 3-inch (7.5 cm) rounds. Reroll scraps gently and cut out more rounds — 24 in total. Fit pastry into 2-inch (5 cm) tart pans. Press dough into pan to take the shape nicely. Prick dough.
3. Bake pastry in a preheated 400°F (200°C) oven for 5 minutes. Cool.
4. Reduce oven temperature to 350°F (180°C). Brush bottom of pastry with Dijon mustard.
5. Meanwhile, heat butter in skillet on medium heat. Add onions and garlic and cook until fragrant and tender. Cool.
6. In bowl, beat eggs with cream, salt, pepper, Tabasco and nutmeg.
7. Place a little onion mixture in each tart. Pour in custard mixture. Sprinkle with green onions. Bake for 15 to 20 minutes, or until custard is just set. Serve warm or at room temperature.

A Lighter Side: Roll pastry very thin and freeze extra for another time. Use milk instead of cream in the filling and cook onions in 1 tbsp (15 mL) oil in a non-stick pan.

Mussels Provençale

When I wrote a story on mussels for *Canadian Living Magazine* years ago, I tested and tasted so many mussel recipes. But this traditional dish is still one of my favorites. Serve it with lots of crusty bread and spoons to slurp up the juices.

This dish has the added bonus of being low in calories.

Serves 6 to 8

4 lb	mussels	2 kg
1 cup	dry white wine	250 mL
1	shallot, finely chopped	1
4	cloves garlic, finely chopped	4
2 tbsp	extra-virgin olive oil	25 mL
1	onion, chopped	1

1	28-oz (796 mL) tin plum tomatoes, drained and chopped	1
1 tbsp	chopped fresh tarragon	15 mL
3 tbsp	chopped fresh parsley	50 mL
	Salt and freshly ground black pepper to taste	
2 tbsp	chopped fresh chives	25 mL

1. Clean mussels well (if you are using cultured mussels, rinse). Pull off beards. Discard any mussels that do not close when shell is lightly tapped, or any mussels that are cracked. Place in large pot and sprinkle with wine, shallots and 1 chopped clove of garlic. Cover and bring to a boil. Simmer for 3 to 5 minutes, or until mussels open. Discard any that do not open. Strain juices through sieve lined with a paper towel and reserve.

2. Meanwhile, heat olive oil in skillet on medium-high heat. Add onions and remaining garlic and cook until tender. Add tomatoes and strained juices from mussels and cook for about 5 minutes. Add tarragon, parsley, salt and pepper.

3. Pour mixture over mussels and toss. Serve in shallow bowls and sprinkle with chives.

BAKING BLIND *Baking "blind" helps keep a bottom crust from getting soggy and bubbling up by precooking the pastry before filling. Line the unbaked pastry shell with parchment paper or foil. Fill with pie weights, dried beans or uncooked rice. Bake for 15 minutes in a preheated 425°F (220°C) oven. Remove the weights and then gently remove the paper. Continue with the recipe. For tarts, use paper muffin cups to line the pastry shells.*

Mussels with Herb Crust

This is a great way to serve mussels for a cocktail party, because the shells make little neat dishes. Otherwise you can serve six to twelve mussels on individual plates as a sit-down first course. Provide lots of crusty bread to soak up any extra juices.

Serves 8 to 12

3 lb	mussels	1.5 kg
1/2 cup	dry white wine	125 mL
1	shallot, coarsely chopped	1
1/3 cup	unsalted butter	75 mL
3	cloves garlic, minced	3
3	shallots, finely chopped	3
1/4 cup	chopped fresh parsley	50 mL
1/4 cup	chopped fresh basil	50 mL
1/4 cup	chopped fresh chives or green onions	50 mL
1 cup	fresh breadcrumbs *(page 25)*	250 mL
1/2 tsp	salt	2 mL
1/2 tsp	freshly ground black pepper	2 mL

1. Scrub mussels well and pull off beards. Discard any mussels that are cracked, heavy or do not close when shells are tapped.
2. Place mussels and wine in a large pot. Sprinkle with coarsely chopped shallot. Cover and bring to a boil. Steam for 5 to 8 minutes, or until mussels open. Discard any mussels that do not open.
3. Strain, freezing juices for another use. Remove top shells, leaving mussels on bottom shells. Place on baking sheet.
4. In saucepan, melt butter. Stir in remaining ingredients. Sprinkle mixture over mussels.
5. Preheat broiler. Broil mussels for 3 to 5 minutes, or until golden and crusty.

A Lighter Side: Use 3 tbsp (50 mL) olive oil instead of 1/3 cup (75 mL) butter.

MUSSELS *You can buy cultured mussels or wild mussels. Pull off the beards before using. Cultured mussels are usually fairly clean when you buy them and only have to be rinsed. Wild mussels are considered by some connaisseurs to be more flavorful than cultured, but they must be scrubbed well before using. Discard any mussels that are cracked, unusually heavy, or that do not close when the shell is lightly tapped.*

Shrimp Mousse in Tarragon Cream Sauce

Before the introduction of the food processor, fish mousse (quenelles) was so laborious and time-consuming to prepare that it was rarely cooked at home. Now it's easy to make this elegant first course.

For the garnish I always try to use homemade tomato sauce to make the swirls, but a famous French chef once taught me a trick — ketchup.

Serves 8

1 lb	shrimp, shelled and cleaned	500 g
2	egg whites	2
1/2 tsp	salt	2 mL
1/4 tsp	freshly ground black pepper	1 mL
1 1/4 cups	whipping cream, cold	300 mL

TARRAGON CREAM SAUCE

1 1/2 cups	whipping cream	375 mL
1/2 tsp	salt	2 mL
2 tbsp	chopped fresh tarragon (or 2 tsp/10 mL dried)	25 mL

GARNISH

8	cooked baby shrimp	8
8	sprigs fresh tarragon	8
1/4 cup	rich tomato sauce or ketchup	50 mL

1. Pat shrimp dry. Cut each shrimp into quarters. Place in food processor fitted with metal blade. Process on/off until finely chopped.
2. Add egg whites and puree until smooth. Add salt and pepper. With machine running, slowly add cream through feed tube. Scrape down sides of bowl and blend in.
3. Butter eight ramekins and line each bottom with a round of parchment paper. Divide mixture among ramekins. Place ramekins in roasting pan filled with hot water to come halfway up the sides of the mousses. (This bain-marie cooks the mousses very gently.)
4. Bake in a preheated 350°F (180°C) oven for 20 minutes, or until firm to the touch.
5. Meanwhile, prepare sauce by bringing cream, salt and dried tarragon (if using) to a boil in saucepan. Cook gently (do not let cream boil over) until reduced and thickened — you should have about 1 1/4 cups (300 mL) sauce in the end. (If you are using fresh tarragon, add it about 3 minutes before sauce is finished.)
6. To serve, unmold mousse by running a knife around outside edge. Invert onto serving plate. Discard parchment paper rounds. Spoon some sauce on each and top with a cooked shrimp and sprig of tarragon.
7. Put tomato sauce in squeeze bottle or Ziploc-type bag and pipe little lines around mousse in the sauce. Swirl with the tip of a knife.

A Lighter Side: Use 3/4 cup (175 mL) cream in the shrimp mixture. Serve with your favorite lightly flavored tomato sauce instead of the cream sauce.

Seafood Sausages

I had this first at a three-star restaurant in Paris. I was impressed with the texture, flavor and presentation of the dish. This is how it went (or pretty close).

Serves 6 to 8

1 lb	firm-fleshed white fish (such as pike or whitefish)	500 g
2	egg whites	2
1 1/2 cups	whipping cream	375 mL
1 tsp	salt	5 mL
1/4 tsp	freshly ground black pepper	1 mL
2 tbsp	finely chopped fresh herbs (combination of parsley, chives and tarragon)	25 mL
8 oz	fresh scallops, finely diced	250 g
8 oz	shrimp, shelled, cleaned and finely diced	250 g
1 1/4 cups	Tarragon Cream Sauce *(page 89)* Sprigs fresh tarragon	300 mL

1. Cut fish into 1-inch (2.5 cm) chunks and pat dry. Place in food processor fitted with metal blade. Chop fish coarsely.
2. Add egg whites and puree until smooth. Slowly, with machine running, drizzle cream through feed tube. Add salt, pepper and herbs. Blend in. Fold in scallops and shrimp.
3. On three pieces of foil or plastic wrap, arrange mixture into three logs and wrap well.
4. Bring 5-inches (12 cm) water to a boil in fish poacher or large deep pan. Add wrapped rolls and submerge. Water should be at 180°F (80°C), just below a boil. Simmer for 30 minutes. Let sausages cool in the water for 10 minutes.
5. To serve, unwrap sausages and cut into slices approximately 3/4 inch (2 cm) thick. Serve with sauce over or under slices. Garnish with sprigs of fresh tarragon or other fresh herbs.

A Lighter Side: Use only 1 cup (250 mL) whipping cream in the sausages. Serve with a lightly flavored tomato sauce instead of the cream sauce.

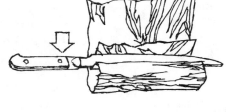

Smoked Salmon Crêpes with Sweet Mustard Sauce

This is an elegant appetizer that is easy to prepare and serve. The crêpes can be made a day or two ahead and filled just before serving. They can be served as an hors d'oeuvre or first course at a formal dinner.

Makes approximately 16 crêpes

CREPES

4	eggs	4
1 cup	all-purpose flour	250 mL
1/2 tsp	salt	2 mL
1 cup	milk	250 mL
1/4 cup	water	50 mL
1/4 cup	unsalted butter, melted	50 mL

SWEET MUSTARD SAUCE

1 cup	sour cream	250 mL
1/2 cup	mayonnaise	125 mL
1/3 cup	Russian-style mustard	75 mL
2 tbsp	chopped fresh dill	25 mL
2 tbsp	tiny capers	25 mL
1/2 tsp	freshly ground black pepper	2 mL
	Salt to taste	
1 tbsp	lemon juice	15 mL
1 lb	smoked salmon, thinly sliced	500 g
	Tiny sprigs fresh dill	

1. Prepare crêpe batter by whisking eggs in bowl with flour and salt. Carefully beat in milk and water. Stir in all but 1 tbsp (15 mL) melted butter. Cover batter and refrigerate for 1 hour.
2. Heat the remaining 1 tbsp (15 mL) butter in an 8-inch (20 cm) crêpe or omelet pan on medium-high heat. (Unsalted burns and sticks less than salted butter.) Make each crêpe by adding a ladleful of batter to hot pan. Swirl it in the pan and pour excess back into bowl of batter. Cook crêpe for 1 minute until brown and then flip. Cook second side until dotted with brown. Remove from pan. Repeat with remaining batter — you should have 12 to 16 crêpes.
3. Prepare sauce by whisking sour cream with mayonnaise and mustard in bowl until smooth. Stir in dill, capers and pepper. Season with salt (only if necessary) and lemon juice.
4. Arrange crêpes on work surface, dotted side up. Spread about 1 1/2 tbsp (20 mL) sauce on each crêpe. Separate salmon slices and arrange one slice on half of each crêpe. Fold crêpe in half over salmon and then into quarters, as shown. Place sprig of dill in each fold.
5. Serve one or two crêpes per person. Drizzle any extra sauce over the top if you wish. You can garnish the plate with a cherry tomato rose *(page 4)* and another sprig of dill.

A Lighter Side: Use skim milk to make crêpe batter. Use low-fat unflavored yogurt instead of sour cream in the sauce; use half the amount of mayonnaise.

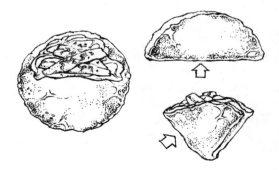

Smoked Salmon Roulade

You can serve this as a sit-down first course, or you can make smaller rolls, slice them thinly and serve them like party sandwiches.

Serves 8 to 10

1/4 cup	unsalted butter	50 mL
1/3 cup	all-purpose flour	75 mL
1 1/2 cups	milk, hot	375 mL
6	eggs, separated	6
1 tsp	salt	5 mL
1/4 tsp	freshly ground black pepper	1 mL
1/4 tsp	cayenne pepper	1 mL
1/4 cup	fine breadcrumbs	50 mL

FILLING

6 oz	herb cream cheese	175 g
	(Boursin, Rondele or *see page 29*) or plain cream cheese	
2 tbsp	sour cream	25 mL
8 oz	thinly sliced smoked salmon	250 g

SAUCE

1 cup	sour cream	250 mL
2 tbsp	mayonnaise	25 mL
1/4 cup	Russian-style mustard	50 mL

1. Butter a large 17 x 12-inch (43 x 30 cm) jellyroll pan and line with parchment paper. Butter again and flour lightly.
2. Melt butter in large saucepan. Whisk in flour and cook over low heat for 5 minutes until flour smells "cooked" but mixture is not brown.
3. Whisk in milk and bring to a boil. Cook for a few minutes until thickened, stirring all the while.
4. In large bowl, beat egg yolks together. Gradually beat in the sauce. Add salt, pepper and cayenne. Mixture should be well seasoned. Cool slightly.
5. In separate bowl, beat egg whites until light but firm. (Do not overbeat.) Stir a little of the whites into the egg yolk mixture and then fold the two mixtures together gently.
6. Spread soufflé mixture evenly over prepared pan. Bake in a preheated 400°F (200°C) oven for 15 to 18 minutes, or until golden.
7. Meanwhile, beat cheese with 2 tbsp (25 mL) sour cream. Reserve.
8. Prepare sauce by combining 1 cup (250 mL) sour cream with mayonnaise and mustard. Reserve each mixture separately.
9. Sprinkle soufflé with breadcrumbs. Cover with clean tea towel. Invert. Carefully remove paper. Trim edges and eat them.
10. Gently spread soufflé with cheese mixture. Arrange slices of salmon on top. Roll up gently along long side. Transfer to serving platter using tea towel to lift roulade.
11. To serve, cut roll into 1-inch (2.5 cm) slices and drizzle each slice with some of the sauce.

A Lighter Side: Use skim milk in the soufflé mixture. Use low-fat pressed cottage cheese blended with low-fat unflavored yogurt instead of cream cheese and sour cream in the filling. For the sauce use low-fat unflavored yogurt instead of the sour cream and half the mayonnaise, or omit sauce completely.

Black Pepper Brioche

Not only does this taste great with the Wild Mushroom Gratin *(page 80)*, this is just your all-round great-tasting bread. It is a perfect base for many spreads and appetizers and a good recipe to have on file. If you want a terrific basic brioche, just leave out the pepper. If you are serving the brioche with dinner, you can bake it in individual fluted brioche pans.

Makes 2 loaves

2 tsp	granulated sugar	10 mL
1/4 cup	warm water	50 mL
1	envelope dry yeast (1 tbsp/15 mL)	1
4 cups	all-purpose flour	1 L
1 1/2 tsp	salt	7 mL
2 tbsp	granulated sugar	25 mL
4 tsp	freshly ground black pepper	20 mL

1/2 cup	milk	125 mL
3	eggs	3
2	egg yolks	2
3/4 cup	unsalted butter, softened	175 mL

GLAZE

1	egg	1
1/2 tsp	salt	2 mL

1. In cup, dissolve 2 tsp (10 mL) sugar in warm water and sprinkle yeast on top. Allow to rest for 10 minutes, or until yeast bubbles up.
2. In large bowl (or bowl of a mixer with a dough hook), combine 2 1/2 cups (625 mL) flour with salt, 2 tbsp (25 mL) sugar and pepper.
3. In separate bowl, beat milk with eggs and yolks. Stir down yeast and add to eggs. Stir egg mixture into flour mixture by hand or with mixer. Dough should be sticky. Beat in soft butter. Add extra flour until dough can just be handled without sticking too much. If mixing by hand, knead for about 5 minutes with floured hands. In mixer, beat for 3 to 4 minutes.
4. Place dough in a buttered bowl (turn dough over to coat with butter), cover with plastic wrap and allow to rise for 1 hour at room temperature, or until dough has doubled in bulk.
5. Punch dough down, knead slightly and place in bowl again. Cover and allow to rise in refrigerator overnight or even a few days if you do not plan to use dough right away. (If you are keeping dough in the refrigerator for a few days, punch it down now and then.)
6. Divide dough in two and shape into loaves. Cover loosely with buttered plastic wrap and allow to rise until doubled in bulk, about 45 to 60 minutes.
7. In small bowl, beat egg and salt together. Brush on top of loaves. Bake in a preheated 375°F (190°C) oven for 40 minutes. Remove from pans and cool on racks.

Black Bean Chili Burritos

Although these are a bit messy to eat, they are so unusual and delicious that no one ever minds. Serve it to good friends wearing casual clothes. Have all the ingredients organized like a buffet and allow everyone to create their own burritos. You can use all or only some of the garnishes — set them out in individual bowls. If you cannot find flour tortillas, just use pita bread.

Serves 16

2 cups	dried black turtle beans	500 mL
2 tbsp	vegetable oil	25 mL
2	onions, chopped	2
4	cloves garlic, finely chopped	4
3 tbsp	chili powder	50 mL
1 tsp	ground cumin	5 mL
1 tsp	paprika	5 mL
1 tsp	dried oregano	5 mL
1	28-oz (796 mL) tin plum tomatoes, pureed with juices	1
3	chipotle *(page 36)* or jalapeño chilies, diced	3
1 tsp	salt	5 mL
1/2 tsp	freshly ground black pepper	2 mL
2 tbsp	chopped fresh coriander	25 mL
16	6-inch (15 cm) flour tortillas	16

GARNISHES
Sour cream, diced avocado, grated Monterey Jack cheese, chopped fresh coriander and/or diced mild green chilies

1. Soak black beans for 3 hours or overnight in enough water to cover generously.
2. Heat oil in Dutch oven on medium-high heat. Add onions and garlic and cook for 5 minutes until tender and fragrant. Add chili powder, cumin, paprika and oregano. Cook for about 30 seconds until well combined.
3. Stir in tomatoes and chipotles. Cook for 10 minutes.
4. Drain beans and add to sauce mixture. Add water if necessary so that beans are covered by about 1-inch (2.5 cm) liquid. Simmer gently for 2 to 3 hours, or until beans are tender and mixture is quite thick. Season with salt, pepper and coriander.
5. Just before serving, warm tortillas by wrapping them in foil and heating in a preheated 350°F (180°C) oven for 10 minutes.
6. Have chili, tortillas and garnishes out on the table. Guests can place some chili in the center of the tortilla, top it with the garnishes they want, and then roll it up to eat.

Potato Pancakes (Latkes)

Of all the little pancakes being served as appetizers and side dishes these days, I think these are still my favorite. Old-fashioned Jewish latkes are crisp and delicious and really in vogue now! Put a little sour cream and caviar or smoked salmon on top, and you have created the ultimate trendy appetizer. Of course, you can eat these at Hannukah, too. My sister, Jane, and I usually make about three hundred for our family Hannukah party. Although they taste best right out of the pan, because of the quantity, we do make them ahead. We stack them upright in rows in a baking dish and reheat them at 400°F (200°C) for 10 to 15 minutes until very hot.

Makes 32 1 1/2-inch (4 cm) pancakes

2	eggs	2
1	small onion, grated	1
3	large baking potatoes, peeled (1 1/2 lb/750 g total)	3
1 tsp	salt	5 mL
1/4 tsp	freshly ground black pepper	1 mL

3 tbsp	cornflake crumbs	50 mL
	Vegetable oil for frying	
	Sour cream	
	Caviar and/or chopped smoked salmon	

1. In large bowl, beat eggs with onion.
2. Finely grate potatoes and combine with egg mixture. (If you are doing this in food processor, chop onion with metal blade, blend in eggs, cut potatoes in chunks and process them with eggs and onions until they are finely chopped. Be careful not to over-process the potatoes. They should be chopped/grated, not pureed.)
3. Blend in salt, pepper and cornflake crumbs.
4. Heat about 1/2-inch (1 cm) oil in large skillet. Add batter by the spoonful and flatten with the back of the spoon. Cook until crisp — 2 to 3 minutes. Turn and cook second side.
5. Drain pancakes on rack or paper towels as they are ready. If you need to add more oil to the pan, add it between batches. Serve hot and preferably freshly cooked, topped with sour cream and caviar and/or smoked salmon.

Potato Pancakes with Shrimp and Dill

This is a wonderful appetizer that can be made ahead and easily reheated. The recipe is based on one from Jean-Pierre Challet, the chef at The Inn at Manitou. I started teaching a series of cooking classes to their guests in 1989, but I also learned a lot from their wonderful chefs. To serve this as a sit-down first course, serve three per plate with a dollop of sour cream and a bit of good caviar.

Makes approximately 30 pancakes

3	potatoes (1 1/4 lb/ 625 g total)	3
3	eggs	3
2/3 cup	all-purpose flour	150 mL
1 tsp	salt	5 mL
1/2 tsp	freshly ground black pepper	2 mL
3 tbsp	unsalted butter, melted	50 mL
1 1/3 cups	light cream (approx.)	325 mL
3 tbsp	unsalted butter (approx.)	50 mL
1 cup	cooked baby shrimp	250 mL
3 tbsp	chopped fresh dill	50 mL

1. Peel potatoes and cut into quarters. Cook in boiling salted water until tender. Drain well and mash smoothly. You should have 2 cups (500 mL).
2. Prepare batter by beating eggs in large bowl. Beat in flour, salt and pepper. Whisk in melted butter and 2/3 cup (150 mL) cream. Whisk in cool mashed potatoes. Add enough additional cream to thin batter to the consistency of thick sour cream.
3. Heat 2 tbsp (25 mL) butter in large skillet on medium-high heat. Spoon about 1 tbsp (15 mL) batter into hot pan for each pancake.
4. Pat shrimp very dry and arrange a few shrimp on the "wet" side of the pancakes. Sprinkle with a little dill. Turn pancakes after 2 minutes and cook second side for 2 to 3 minutes. Be sure pancakes are well cooked. Repeat with remaining batter, adding more butter to skillet as needed.
5. Serve immediately or reheat by placing pancakes in a single layer on baking sheet. Reheat at 400°F (200°C) for 4 to 5 minutes.

A Lighter Side: Use milk instead of cream in batter.

Sweet Pepper Pancakes with Avocado Salsa

These sweet little pancakes just melt in your mouth. You can serve them with drinks or on a plate for a sit-down first course, or you can even make the pancakes into crêpes and roll them around some of the avocado salsa.

Serves 6 to 8

2	eggs	2
1/2 cup	milk	125 mL
1	sweet red pepper, roasted peeled and diced	1
1/2 tsp	salt	2 mL
pinch	freshly ground black pepper	pinch
3/4 cup	all-purpose flour	175 mL
1/4 cup	yellow cornmeal	50 mL
2 tbsp	unsalted butter, melted	25 mL
1/4 cup	unsalted butter (approx.)	50 mL

AVOCADO SALSA

1/4	red onion, diced	1/4
1/2	tomato, seeded and diced	1/2
2 tbsp	chopped mild green chilies (tinned)	25 mL
2 tbsp	chopped fresh coriander	25 mL
1 tsp	white wine vinegar	5 mL
1 tbsp	vegetable oil	15 mL
1/4 tsp	salt	1 mL
1/4 tsp	freshly ground black pepper	1 mL
1	ripe avocado	1

1. In bowl, blend the eggs, milk, red pepper, salt and pepper together with a whisk.
2. In small bowl, combine flour and cornmeal. Stir into batter. Add melted butter. Allow batter to rest, covered, for 30 minutes.
3. Meanwhile, prepare salsa. Soak onion in ice water for 15 minutes. Drain well and pat dry.
4. In bowl, combine tomatoes, chilies, coriander, vinegar, oil, onions, salt and pepper. Dice avocado *(page 20)* and add to tomato mixture. Mash slightly if you want the salsa to hold together a bit more.
5. Cover salsa with plastic wrap, pressing wrap onto surface of mixture until ready to use.
6. To make pancakes, on medium-high heat, heat just enough butter to coat bottom of large skillet. Drop in spoonfuls of batter to make pancakes 2 inches (5 cm) in diameter. Cook for 1 to 2 minutes until browned, flip and cook second side. Repeat with remaining batter, adding more butter to skillet as needed. (These can be made a few hours in advance, held at room temperature and then reheated in a single layer on baking sheets at 375°F/190°C for 5 to 8 minutes.) Serve each pancake with a spoonful of salsa in the center.

5

Soups

Chicken Stock

Although you do not have to use homemade stock in the soups in this book, making your own chicken stock is quick and easy, and your soups will reflect the quality of the stock you use. The better the chicken, the better your home-made stock will be. (We cook with free-range chickens and then use the wings, backs and necks to make stock.) Do not use chicken livers, as they can discolor the stock. If you use a whole chicken to make stock, the meat can be used for salads and sandwiches, but most of its flavor and goodness will be in the stock. Do not add salt to stock until it is used in a recipe. That way, if you are prepar-ing a sauce that must be reduced, the stock will not be too salty.

If you do not have a lot of room in your freezer, cook down the stock to about 4 cups (1 L) and freeze it in ice cube trays — making your own frozen bouillon cubes. When it comes time to use them, simply dilute with boiling water.

Makes approximately 12 cups (3 L)

4 lb	raw chicken pieces	2 kg
16 cups	cold water (approx.)	4 L
2	onions, coarsely chopped	2
2	carrots, sliced	2
2	ribs celery, sliced	2
2	leeks, sliced	2

BOUQUET GARNI		
1	bay leaf	1
1/2 tsp	dried thyme	2 mL
6	whole peppercorns	6
1	small handful fresh parsley	1

1. Place chicken in large pot. Add enough cold water to cover chicken by about 2 inches (5 cm). Bring to a boil. Skim off scum that rises to the surface.
2. Add vegetables and bring to a boil again, skimming again if necessary.
3. Meanwhile, tie ingredients for bou-quet garni together in a little cheese-cloth bag. Add to stock mixture.
4. Reduce heat and allow stock to cook gently, uncovered, for 1 1/2 to 2 hours. Replace water if too much seems to evaporate as stock cooks. Water level should remain at least 1 inch (2.5 cm) above bones.
5. Strain stock and cool. Refrigerate overnight. Remove fat and discard. Refrigerate stock for a few days or freeze for up to 3 months.

Classic Brown Stock

Although brown stock takes a long time to make, most of this is cooking time, when the stock can virtually be left unattended. And you can make a large batch and freeze it, so you don't have to make it often.

Makes 16 cups (4 L)

3 lb	beef bones, cut into 2-inch (5 cm) pieces	1.5 kg		3	ribs celery, cut into chunks	3
3 lb	veal bones, cut into 2-inch (5 cm) pieces	1.5 kg		2	leeks, cut into quarters	2
3 lb	chicken, cut into 2-inch (5 cm) pieces	1.5 kg		3	large tomatoes, cut into chunks	3
4	large onions, unpeeled and cut up	4		2	bay leaves	2
4	large carrots, cut into chunks	4		1/2 tsp	dried thyme	2 mL
				6	whole peppercorns	6

1. Place bones and chicken in a single layer in large roasting pan. Roast in a preheated 425°F (220°C) oven for 1 1/2 hours, turning once halfway through roasting time.
2. Add onions and carrots and brown for another 30 minutes.
3. Remove bones, chicken and vegetables to large stockpot and discard fat. Add about 2 cups (500 mL) water to roasting pan and scrape any bits of solidified juices off bottom of pan. Add these juices to stockpot. Add cold water just to cover bones and vegetables and bring to a boil. Skim any scum that appears on the surface.
4. Add remaining vegetables and seasonings. Simmer gently, uncovered, for 8 to 10 hours or overnight. Water level should remain approximately the same — add more if necessary.
5. Strain stock. Place in a clean pot and reduce to 16 cups (4 L). Refrigerate overnight. Remove fat and discard. Refrigerate stock for a few days or freeze for up to 3 months.

STOCK SUBSTITUTES   *If you don't have homemade chicken or brown stock, frozen salt-free commercial stock is available. I prefer canned bouillon over bouillon cubes, but both can be extremely salty, so be sure to dilute them much more than the package recommends, and taste the dish before adding extra salt.*

Lentil Soup with Chèvre Cream

I knew lentil soup was becoming the rage when I had a dinner party for five guests, and two of them had had lentil soup for lunch. What did I do? I told them they were having it again!

When making soup, I like to use the little red lentils (sometimes called pink or orange), as they cook faster and practically dissolve with tenderness. They turn a murky brown color when cooked, so don't be surprised.

Serves 8

2 tbsp	extra-virgin olive oil	25 mL
1	onion, chopped	1
2	cloves garlic, finely chopped	2
pinch	hot red chili flakes	pinch
1 tsp	ground cumin	5 mL
1 1/2 cups	dried red lentils, rinsed and picked over	375 mL
1	potato, peeled and finely diced	1
6 cups	chicken stock or water	1.5 L
	Salt and freshly ground black pepper to taste	

CHÈVRE CREAM

2 oz	chèvre (creamy mild goat cheese)	60 g
1/2 cup	whipping cream	125 mL
2 tbsp	chopped fresh coriander (optional)	25 mL

1. Heat oil in large saucepan or Dutch oven on medium-high heat. Cook onion, garlic and chili flakes for 3 to 5 minutes until fragrant.
2. Add cumin and cook for 30 seconds. Stir in lentils and potato and combine well.
3. Add stock, a little salt and pepper if stock is unseasoned and bring to a boil. Reduce heat and simmer gently until lentils and potatoes are tender and beginning to thicken, about 25 to 30 minutes.
4. Meanwhile, prepare chèvre cream. Crumble cheese into cream in small heavy saucepan and warm gently. Cook for a few minutes until smooth and creamy. Cool slightly.
5. Puree soup if you wish, and return it to saucepan. Add water or stock to thin soup if necessary. Taste and adjust seasoning.
6. To serve, ladle soup into shallow bowls. Pour chèvre cream into a squeeze bottle or Ziploc-type bag and drizzle on soup in a zigzag design. Sprinkle with coriander if you wish.

A Lighter Side: Omit the cream and cheese garnish.

White Bean Soup with Prosciutto

It's amazing how times have changed. Not only is a bean soup now elegant enough for a fancy dinner party, it's so delicious that no one will believe you are serving beans! For the dried beans, you can substitute two 19-oz (540 mL) tins white beans, drained and rinsed. Add them with the potatoes after cooking the onions and garlic. Then the soup will only take 25 to 30 minutes to cook.

Serves 8

1 1/4 cups	dried white kidney beans	300 mL
2 tbsp	extra-virgin olive oil	25 mL
1	onion, chopped	1
3	cloves garlic, finely chopped	3
pinch	hot red chili flakes	pinch
1 tsp	ground cumin	5 mL
1	potato, peeled and diced	1
6 cups	chicken stock or water	1.5 L
	Salt and freshly ground black pepper to taste	
1/2 cup	whipping cream	125 mL
1 tbsp	lemon juice	15 mL
	Tabasco sauce to taste	
4 oz	prosciutto, sliced 1/8 inch (3 mm) thick and cut into julienne	125 g
2 tbsp	chopped fresh coriander or parsley	25 mL

1. Rinse beans and remove any foreign particles. Place beans in large bowl and cover with cold water. Allow to soak for a few hours or overnight. Drain well.
2. Heat oil in Dutch oven or large saucepan over medium-high heat. Cook onion, garlic and chili flakes for 5 to 8 minutes, until fragrant and tender.
3. Add cumin and cook for 30 seconds. Stir in drained beans, potato and stock. Bring to a boil, reduce heat and cook gently until beans are tender, 1 to 1 1/2 hours.
4. Puree soup and return to saucepan. (Puree just half the soup, if you wish, for a coarser texture.) Season with salt and pepper and add cream. Heat thoroughly. If soup is too thick, add chicken stock or water. Season with lemon juice and Tabasco.
5. To serve, place soup in bowls and mound shredded ham in the center of each bowl. Sprinkle with coriander.

A Lighter Side: Omit the whipping cream.

Butternut Squash Soup with Gorgonzola Cream

I love butternut squash. Although it is slightly more expensive than the others, it is much more buttery, seems to be less watery in texture and has a very sweet taste.

It's a bonus if you can find squash that is already peeled, because it is very hard and a little difficult to peel yourself.

Serves 8

3 tbsp	unsalted butter	50 mL		1 tsp	chopped fresh thyme (or pinch dried)	5 mL
2	leeks (white and light-green parts only), cleaned and thinly sliced	2		1 tsp	chopped fresh rosemary (or pinch dried)	5 mL
1	small clove garlic, finely chopped	1		1/2 cup	whipping cream	125 mL
1 1/2 lb	butternut squash, peeled and diced	750 g			Salt and freshly ground black pepper to taste	
1	pear or apple, peeled, cored and diced	1				
1	potato, peeled and diced	1		GORGONZOLA CREAM		
4 cups	chicken stock	1 L		1/2 cup	whipping cream	125 mL
				4 oz	Gorgonzola cheese	125 g

1. Melt butter in large saucepan or Dutch oven on medium-high heat. Cook leeks and garlic for a few minutes until wilted and fragrant, but do not brown.
2. Add squash, pear or apple and potato. Combine well and cook for 5 minutes.
3. Add chicken stock, thyme and rosemary. Bring to a boil, cover, reduce heat and simmer gently for 30 to 40 minutes, until squash is very tender.

4. Puree soup, return to saucepan, reheat and stir in cream. Taste and add salt and pepper.
5. While soup is cooking, in small saucepan, heat cream for garnish and stir in cheese. Cook, stirring constantly, until smooth. Cool.
6. Serve soup in shallow bowls with a swirl of Gorgonzola cream.

A Lighter Side: Start leeks in half the amount of butter. Omit the cream and cheese garnish.

COOKING WITH WINE *If you stocked every wine or liqueur that was called for in a modern cookbook or food magazine, you would have a cupboard full. But you can get by with a few essentials. Have a reasonably priced but good-quality dry white and red wine for cooking. Once the wine has been opened, pour a little olive oil into the bottle to protect the wine from the air and refrigerate it. The wine can be used for cooking for a few months. I also keep a brandy or Cognac on hand to use in savory dishes and desserts. Although sherry, Port and Marsala are all nice to have, you can usually use a little Cognac or brandy instead.*

Mussel Soup

You could serve this as an appetizer or as a light summer meal with salad and bread.

Serves 8 to 10

4 lb	mussels, cleaned	2 kg
1 cup	dry white wine	250 mL
1 tbsp	chopped fresh tarragon (or 1/2 tsp/2 mL dried)	15 mL
1 tbsp	chopped fresh parsley	15 mL
1	shallot, chopped	1
3 tbsp	unsalted butter	50 mL
6 oz	bacon, diced	175 g
6	cloves garlic, finely chopped	6
3	leeks (white and light-green parts only), cleaned and chopped	3
1	potato, peeled and diced	1
3	carrots, peeled and chopped	3
4 cups	fish stock or chicken stock	1 L
1 cup	whipping cream or crème fraîche (*page 11*)	250 mL
	Salt and freshly ground black pepper to taste	
3 tbsp	chopped fresh parsley	50 mL
2 tbsp	chopped fresh chives or green onions	25 mL

1. Place cleaned mussels in large pot and sprinkle with wine, tarragon, 1 tbsp (15 mL) parsley and shallot. Cover and bring to a boil. Reduce heat and simmer for 3 to 5 minutes, or until mussels open. Cool.
2. Meanwhile, heat butter in Dutch oven or large saucepan on medium-high heat. Add diced bacon and cook until crisp. Discard all but about 1/4 cup (50 mL) fat from the pan. Add garlic, leeks, potatoes and carrots. Cook until very tender, about 15 minutes. Add stock and bring to a boil. Cook for 15 minutes.
3. When mussels are cool enough to handle, remove from shells, saving all the cooking liquid and juices. Reserve mussels and strain liquid. Add liquid to soup. Cook for 10 minutes.
4. Add cream and heat thoroughly. Add mussels and heat through. Season to taste with salt and lots of pepper. Sprinkle with 3 tbsp (50 mL) parsley and chives.

A Lighter Side: Omit the bacon and cream. Use an additional 1 cup (250 mL) stock. Use 4 tsp (20 mL) olive oil instead of the butter.

Grilled Chicken and Vegetable Soup

The smoky taste of this soup is unexpected and different. Without the cheese and olive oil it is very low-cal.

Serves 8 to 10

3	tomatoes	3
2	zucchini	2
2	sweet red peppers	2
2	sweet yellow peppers	2
2	hot banana peppers	2
2	red onions	2
1	head garlic	1
8 oz	small red potatoes	250 g
1/4 cup	extra-virgin olive oil (optional)	50 mL
1 lb	boneless, skinless chicken breasts	500 g

5 cups	chicken stock	1.25 L
1/4 cup	lemon juice	50 mL
1 tsp	ground cumin	5 mL
1 tsp	ground coriander	5 mL
1	bunch fresh coriander	1
	Salt and freshly ground black pepper to taste	
1 cup	crumbled feta cheese (about 8 oz/250 g)	250 mL
1/2 cup	chopped fresh coriander	125 mL

1. Heat barbecue. Brush grill with olive oil. Place tomatoes on grill and turn as they blacken. Halve zucchini and grill. Turn to grill the other side. Place whole peppers on grill and turn as they darken. Peel onions and cut in half. Grill onions on both sides. Cut top (pointed end) and papery skin off garlic and grill whole. Scrub potatoes, cut in half and grill. Brush vegetables with olive oil during cooking if you wish. The vegetables do not have to be completely cooked — you just want to impart a smoky flavor.
2. As vegetables are ready, transfer them to baking sheet to cool.
3. Grill chicken for about 3 minutes per side. Cool and slice thinly.
4. Meanwhile, combine chicken stock, lemon juice, cumin and ground coriander in large saucepan or Dutch oven and bring to a boil.
5. Peel tomatoes and dice. Slice zucchini. Remove skins from peppers. Halve and seed them and slice into strips. Dice onions. Leave garlic bulb whole. Cut potatoes into large cubes. Add all vegetables to stock. Leave coriander tied in a bunch and add to soup so it can be removed at end. Add chicken slices.
6. Cook soup for 30 minutes until vegetables are tender. Remove garlic and coriander. Taste soup and adjust seasoning with salt and pepper.
7. To serve, sprinkle with cheese and chopped fresh coriander.

A Lighter Side: Omit the olive oil and feta cheese.

Winter Root Vegetable Soup with Cheddar

I like using a combination of root vegetables for this soup, but if you do not have all the ones listed below, use any combination.

Serves 6 to 8

2 tbsp	unsalted butter or vegetable oil	25 mL
1	onion, chopped	1
2	cloves garlic, finely chopped	2
1	potato, peeled and diced	1
3 cups	diced (peeled) root vegetables such as carrots, parsnips, turnips, squash and/ or sweet potatoes	750 mL
4 cups	chicken stock	1 L
	Salt and freshly ground black pepper to taste	
3 tbsp	chopped fresh dill or parsley	50 mL
1/2 cup	grated Cheddar cheese (about 2 oz/60 g)	125 mL

1. Heat butter or oil in large saucepan or Dutch oven on medium-high heat. Add onion and garlic and cook for a few minutes until fragrant and tender.
2. Stir in potato and diced vegetables. Add stock and bring to a boil.
3. Reduce heat, cover and simmer gently for 20 minutes, or until vegetables are tender.
4. Puree soup and return to saucepan to heat thoroughly. (Depending on the vegetables you have used, the soup may be too thick. If so, simply add a little stock or water.) Taste soup and season with salt and pepper if necessary.
5. Serve sprinkled with a little fresh dill and cheese.

BARBECUING AND GRILLING *The terms barbecuing and grilling are often used interchangeably these days. Not only are people grilling outside, many cooks have indoor gas or electric grills, or the new smokeless portable grills. Grilling is popular because it is an easy, low-fat cooking method. Preheat the grill for about 10 to 15 minutes before using (a charcoal fire will take about 30 minutes) and brush the grill with olive oil about 1 minute before putting the food on. This helps prevent sticking and helps give the food decorative grill markings.*

If you do not have a grill, use a broiler; it won't add a smoky flavor to your food, but it is an adequate substitute.

Corn Soup with Red Pepper Paint

Pipe the red pepper paint on the soup in Southwestern designs (page 7).

Serves 8

3 tbsp	unsalted butter	50 mL
1	small onion, finely chopped	1
1	clove garlic, finely chopped	1
4 cups	fresh or frozen corn niblets (about 8 ears)	1 L
1	potato, peeled and diced	1
3 cups	milk	750 mL
1 1/2 cups	light cream	375 mL

1 tsp	salt	5 mL
1/4 tsp	freshly ground black pepper	1 mL

RED PEPPER PAINT

1	sweet red pepper	1
1	chipotle chili *(page 36)*	1
1 tbsp	adobo sauce (comes with chipotles)	15 mL

1. Heat butter in large saucepan or Dutch oven on medium-high heat. Cook onion and garlic until tender and fragrant. Add corn and cook for a few minutes.
2. Add potato and milk. Bring to a boil, reduce heat and cook gently for 20 to 25 minutes, or until potatoes are tender. Puree.
3. Return soup to saucepan. Add cream, salt and pepper and heat. Taste and adjust seasonings if necessary.
4. Meanwhile, broil red pepper until black and blistered on all sides. Cool. Remove black peel. Discard ribs and seeds.
5. Puree pepper with chipotle chili and adobo sauce. If mixture is too thick, thin with a little water or stock. Place mixture in a squirt bottle or piping tube. (Mixture should be consistency of thick paint and should taste very piquant.)
6. To serve, spoon soup into individual shallow soup bowls. Pipe a little paint onto soup.

A Lighter Side: Use half the butter. Use chicken stock instead of the milk and cream.

ROASTING PEPPERS *Roast whole peppers on the barbecue, or place them on a baking sheet and grill them under the broiler about 4 inches (10 cm) from the heat, until the peppers are charred on all sides (turn them every 5 minutes). When the peppers are cool, remove the charred skin. Discard the stem, seeds and ribs. The peppers can be frozen (before or after peeling), so roast lots when they are in season and reasonably priced.*

Grilled Red Pepper Soup with Herbed Chèvre Quenelles

This is a barbecued soup with wonderful little "dumplings" as the garnish. The quenelle mixture also makes a great spread for bread or toast. Little rounds of toast spread with the chèvre mixture can be floated on soup or be used to top a salad.

Serves 6

6	large sweet red peppers	6
1	red onion, cut into thick slices	1
3 tbsp	unsalted butter	50 mL
2	cloves garlic, finely chopped	2
pinch	hot red chili flakes	pinch
2 cups	chicken stock	500 mL
	Salt and freshly ground black pepper to taste	
1/2 cup	whipping cream	125 mL

HERBED CHÈVRE QUENELLES

8 oz	chèvre (creamy mild goat cheese)	250 g
1	small clove garlic, minced	1
2 tbsp	chopped fresh parsley	25 mL
2 tbsp	chopped fresh basil	25 mL
1 tsp	chopped fresh rosemary (or 1/4 tsp/1 mL dried)	5 mL
1/4 tsp	freshly ground black pepper	1 mL
2	sun-dried tomatoes, finely chopped	2

1. Heat barbecue or broiler. Grill peppers on all sides until blackened. Allow to cool. Peel off blackened skin. Halve peppers, discard seeds and stems and chop coarsely. Grill onion slices and dice.
2. Melt butter in large saucepan or Dutch oven on medium-high heat. Add onion and garlic. Cook for a few minutes until tender and fragrant. Add chili flakes. Cook for 1 minute.
3. Add red peppers, stock and a little salt and pepper. Cook for about 10 minutes.
4. Puree soup and return to saucepan. Stir in cream and heat. Taste and adjust seasoning with salt and pepper.
5. While soup is cooking, prepare quenelles. In bowl, beat cheese until smooth. Beat in remaining ingredients. Shape cheese into small ovals to imitate quenelles.
6. To serve, ladle soup into shallow soup bowls. Place two or three quenelles in each.

A Lighter Side: Use chicken stock instead of cream. Substitute low-fat pressed cottage cheese for half of the chèvre. Use half the butter.

Oyster and Corn Bisque

We feature this soup in a holiday entertaining course, but you can bring a holiday feeling to your table any time you serve this.

Serves 8 to 10

3 tbsp	unsalted butter	50 mL
2	leeks (white and light-green parts only), cleaned and thinly sliced	2
2	cloves garlic, finely chopped	2
1	sweet red pepper, peeled, seeded and diced	1
2	potatoes, peeled and diced	2
2 cups	milk	500 mL
1/2 tsp	salt	2 mL
1/4 tsp	freshly ground black pepper	1 mL
2 cups	fresh or frozen corn niblets (about 4 ears)	500 mL
1 cup	whipping cream	250 mL
3 cups	shucked oysters (about 36)	750 mL
2 tbsp	chopped fresh parsley	25 mL

1. Melt butter in Dutch oven or large saucepan on medium-high heat. Add leeks and garlic. Cook gently for 5 minutes until very fragrant and tender. Add red peppers and cook gently for 5 minutes longer.
2. Add potatoes and combine well. Add milk, salt and pepper. Bring to a boil, reduce heat and simmer gently until potatoes are almost tender, about 10 minutes. Add corn and cook for 10 minutes longer.
3. Add cream and heat thoroughly.
4. Meanwhile, place oysters with their juices in small saucepan. Heat gently until edges of oysters just begin to curl. Skim mixture if any froth rises to the surface.
5. Add oysters and their juices to soup. Cook very gently for 2 minutes. Taste and adjust seasoning with salt and pepper if necessary. If soup is too thick, add hot milk or cream (to prevent oysters from overcooking).
6. Serve in shallow soup bowls sprinkled with parsley.

A Lighter Side: Reduce butter by half and use chicken stock instead of the milk and whipping cream.

Split Pea Soup with Dill

This is one of my favorite earthy soups. If you prepare it the day before, it will be quite thick. Simply thin with water when you reheat it.

Serves 8 to 10

3 tbsp	unsalted butter or vegetable oil	50 mL
2	onions, diced	2
2	cloves garlic, finely chopped	2
2	carrots, peeled and diced	2
2	parsnips, peeled and diced	2
1	large potato, peeled and diced	1
1 cup	dried split green peas, rinsed and picked over	250 mL
8 cups	chicken stock or water	2 L
1 cup	broken dry thin spaghetti or egg noodles	250 mL
	Salt and freshly ground black pepper to taste	
1/3 cup	chopped fresh dill	75 mL

1. Heat butter or oil in large saucepan or Dutch oven on medium-high heat. Cook onions and garlic for 5 minutes, or until fragrant and tender. Do not brown. Add carrots, parsnips and potatoes and combine well. Cook for another 5 minutes.
2. Add peas and stock. Bring to a boil, reduce heat and simmer gently, covered, for 1 hour, or until peas are tender.
3. Puree half the soup and return to the saucepan. Add the spaghetti and cook for 10 to 15 minutes until pasta is very tender. If soup is too thick, thin with water or stock.
4. Season with salt and pepper. Sprinkle each serving with dill.

ONIONS   *Before using onions raw in a salad, try soaking them in ice water for 30 minutes to make them more mild-tasting. Bermuda onions are very sweet and great in salads; and the Vidalia onion is the sweet onion that everyone is raving about these days.*

For cooking, do not use onions that are too sweet. I usually use white, yellow or red onions.

When chopping onions, use a very sharp knife. Dull knives squeeze out the juice, which often causes people to cry.

Leek and Potato Soup

This old-fashioned favorite is just as good as ever. It can also be completely or partially pureed before serving. (I prefer to use a food mill to puree soups that have potatoes in them, as it won't over process the potatoes.) When served cold, this soup is called Vichyssoise. Personally, I like it hot.

Serves 6 to 8

2 tbsp	unsalted butter	25 mL
3	leeks (white and light-green parts only), cleaned and sliced	3
3	potatoes, peeled and diced	3
3 cups	chicken stock	750 mL
	Salt and freshly ground black pepper to taste	
1 tsp	chopped fresh thyme (or 1/4 tsp/1 mL dried)	5 mL
1/2 cup	light cream	125 mL
2 tbsp	chopped fresh chives, green onions or parsley	25 mL

1. Melt butter in large saucepan or Dutch oven on medium-high heat. Add leeks and cook for 5 to 10 minutes, until they are wilted and very fragrant.
2. Add diced potatoes and combine well. Add stock, salt, pepper and thyme. Bring to a boil. Reduce heat. Cover and simmer gently for 20 minutes, or until potatoes are very tender.
3. Add cream and heat thoroughly. Taste and adjust seasoning if necessary. To serve, sprinkle with chives, green onions or parsley.

A Lighter Side: Omit the cream.

Tomato Soup Cappuccino Style

To cut down on the richness of cream soups, omit or reduce the amount of cream and float a "rich" layer of frothed milk on the surface of the soup instead. If you have an espresso machine, you can froth the milk easily. But if not, you can achieve the same results by frothing a glass of milk with an immersion blender or milkshake machine and then heating it up in a microwave. (Only fill the container one-third full, so it has lots of room to froth.)

Serves 6 to 8

2 tbsp	unsalted butter or extra-virgin olive oil	25 mL
1	onion, chopped	1
2	cloves garlic, finely chopped	2
1	carrot, peeled and diced	1
1	rib celery, diced	1
3 tbsp	all-purpose flour	50 mL
1	28-oz (796 mL) tin plum tomatoes, with juices	1

1 1/2 cups	chicken stock	375 mL
1 cup	milk	250 mL
1/2 cup	light cream or whipping cream	125 mL
	Salt and freshly ground black pepper to taste	

GARNISH

1 cup	milk	250 mL

1. Melt butter or oil in large saucepan or Dutch oven on medium-high heat. Add onion, garlic, carrot and celery. Cook for 10 minutes until tender.
2. Stir in flour and cook for a few minutes.
3. Stir in tomatoes and chicken stock. Break tomatoes up with a spoon. Bring to a boil, reduce heat and simmer, covered, for 20 minutes.
4. Puree soup and return to saucepan. Stir in milk and cream. Heat thoroughly. Season with salt and pepper.

5. For garnish, froth milk as for cappuccino or as described above. Pour some milk into each bowl of soup, allowing the froth to float on the surface. Use more milk if necessary.

A Lighter Side: Use 1 1/2 cups (375 mL) extra chicken stock instead of the milk and cream in the soup.

SALT AND PEPPER   *I like to use sea salt or kosher salt. You can buy it finely ground to use as table salt, or coarsely ground to use in cooking. And always use freshly ground pepper. It makes a world of difference.*

Broccoli Soup with Mustard Parsley Croutons

French onion soup isn't the only one that can have a big crouton.

Serves 6 to 8

2 tbsp	unsalted butter or vegetable oil	25 mL
1	small onion, finely chopped	1
1	clove garlic, finely chopped	1
1	bunch broccoli, trimmed and cut into 2-inch (5 cm) chunks	1
1	potato, peeled and diced	1
2 1/2 cups	chicken stock	625 mL
1/2 cup	whipping cream	125 mL
1 cup	grated Cheddar cheese (about 4 oz/125 g)	250 mL

1 tbsp	Dijon mustard	15 mL
	Salt and freshly ground black pepper to taste	

MUSTARD PARSLEY CROUTONS

6	slices French or Italian bread	6
2 tbsp	unsalted butter	25 mL
2 tbsp	vegetable oil	25 mL
2 tbsp	Dijon mustard	25 mL
1/4 cup	chopped fresh parsley	50 mL

1. Heat butter or oil in large saucepan or Dutch oven on medium-high heat. Cook onion and garlic until tender and fragrant but do not brown.
2. Add broccoli, potatoes and stock. Bring to a boil. Cover and reduce heat. Cook gently for 20 to 25 minutes, until broccoli and potatoes are tender.
3. Puree soup and return to saucepan. Add cream, cheese and mustard. Cook gently until heated thoroughly, cheese has melted and soup is smooth. Season with salt and pepper.

4. Meanwhile, to make croutons, cut bread into 3-inch (7.5 cm) circles. Heat butter and oil in large skillet on medium-high heat and brown bread on both sides until golden. Drain on paper towels. Spread one side of croutons generously with mustard. Dip mustard side into parsley.
5. Serve soup in shallow soup bowls with mustard parsley crouton floating on each portion, parsley side up.

A Lighter Side: Omit the cream and the cheese. Use more chicken stock if necessary. Toast the bread without any butter or oil.

Roasted Eggplant Soup with Herb Swirls

No one ever thinks of putting eggplant into a soup, but it is delicious, so try it. The soup is even better if you can barbecue the eggplant instead of roasting it to add a smoky taste. Use a herb cream cheese or chèvre quenelle mixture *(page 107)*.

Serves 6 to 8

3	eggplants (1 lb/ 500 g each)	3
3 tbsp	extra-virgin olive oil	50 mL
3	red onions, chopped	3
4	cloves garlic, finely chopped	4
3 1/2 cups	chicken stock	875 mL
	Salt and freshly ground black pepper to taste	
1/2 cup	whipping cream	125 mL

HERB SWIRLS

4 oz	herb cream cheese (e.g. Boursin or Rondele, or see *page 29*)	125 g
3 tbsp	light cream or milk	50 mL

1. Pierce eggplant in three or four places and barbecue until skin blackens, turning often. Or microwave *(page 46)* or roast at 425°F (220°C) on baking sheet until skin blisters, about 20 to 30 minutes. Cool, peel and dice.
2. Heat oil in large saucepan or Dutch oven on medium-high heat. Add onions and garlic. Cook without browning until vegetables are very fragrant, about 10 minutes. Add eggplant and cook for 5 minutes longer.
3. Add stock, salt and pepper. Reduce heat, cover and simmer gently for 20 minutes.

4. Puree soup, return to saucepan and stir in whipping cream. Heat thoroughly and adjust seasonings to taste.
5. Meanwhile, beat cheese with light cream in small bowl. Whisk until smooth.
6. Serve soup in shallow soup bowls and swirl some herb cream into each.

A Lighter Side: Instead of stirring whipping cream into the eggplant puree, thin soup with extra stock if necessary. Omit swirls and garnish soup with Red Pepper Paint (page 106).

Oriental Lemon Shrimp and Noodle Soup

The flavors in this soup are exotic, but it is easy to make, and its delicate tastes appeal to all. If you cannot find thin rice vermicelli noodles, use very thin egg/flour vermicelli.

Serves 8

4 oz	thin rice vermicelli noodles	125 g
2 tbsp	vegetable oil	25 mL
2	cloves garlic, finely chopped	2
1 tbsp	finely chopped fresh ginger root	15 mL
pinch	hot red chili flakes	pinch
1 tsp	grated lemon peel	5 mL
4 cups	chicken or fish stock	1 L
3 tbsp	lemon juice	50 mL
1 tbsp	soy sauce	15 mL

12 oz	shrimp, shelled, cleaned and diced	375 g
1/2 tsp	oriental sesame oil	2 mL
3	green onions, chopped	3
1/3 cup	chopped fresh coriander or parsley	75 mL
2 tbsp	chopped fresh mint	25 mL
2 tbsp	chopped fresh basil	25 mL
	Salt and freshly ground black pepper to taste	

1. Break noodles into 2-inch (5 cm) lengths. Place in bowl and cover with boiling water. Allow to stand for 10 minutes. Drain well and rinse with cold water.
2. In large saucepan or Dutch oven, heat oil on medium-high heat. Add garlic, ginger, chili flakes and lemon peel. Cook for 1 to 2 minutes until very fragrant, but do not brown.
3. Add chicken stock, lemon juice and soy sauce. Bring to a boil. Cook gently for 5 minutes.
4. Add shrimp and noodles. Cook for 3 to 5 minutes, until shrimp are cooked and noodles are heated through.
5. Stir in sesame oil, green onions, coriander, mint and basil. Season with salt and pepper.

Pacific Scallop Soup

This is a gently flavored oriental soup. You can use lean white-fleshed fish fillets, shelled shrimp or boneless, skinless chicken breasts instead of the scallops. The scallop mixture can also be poached or deep-fried and served with a dipping sauce.

Serves 6 to 8

1 tsp	vegetable oil	5 mL
2	cloves garlic, finely chopped	2
1 tbsp	finely chopped fresh ginger root	15 mL
1 tsp	grated lemon peel	5 mL
1/4 tsp	hot red chili flakes	1 mL
4 cups	chicken stock	1 L
2 tbsp	Thai fish sauce or soy sauce	25 mL
1 tbsp	lemon juice	15 mL
1/2 tsp	oriental sesame oil	2 mL
3	carrots, sliced into flower shapes *(page 5)*	3
4	green onions, finely chopped	4

SCALLOP BALLS

1	clove garlic, cut in half	1
1	1/2-inch (1 cm) piece ginger, cut into quarters	1
1 tbsp	rice wine or mirin	15 mL
1 tbsp	water	15 mL
1 tbsp	cornstarch	15 mL
1/4 tsp	oriental sesame oil	1 mL
1/4 tsp	salt	1 mL
8 oz	fresh scallops or whitefish, cleaned	250 g
1	egg white	1
2 tbsp	chopped fresh coriander	25 mL

1. In large saucepan or Dutch oven, heat oil on medium heat. Add garlic, ginger, lemon peel and chili flakes. Cook gently for a few minutes until very fragrant.
2. Add chicken stock, fish sauce, lemon juice and sesame oil. Bring to a boil. Add carrots. Reduce heat and simmer gently for 15 minutes while preparing scallops.
3. To make scallop balls, place garlic and ginger in small dish. Add rice wine and water. Allow to soak for 5 minutes. Drain well. Discard garlic and ginger and reserve liquid in small bowl.
4. Stir cornstarch, sesame oil and salt into reserved liquid.
5. Cut up scallops and place in food processor fitted with the metal blade. Chop. Add cornstarch liquid and egg white. Puree until smooth.
6. Fill large shallow saucepan with 3 inches (7.5 cm) water and bring to a boil. Drop scallop mixture into water in small balls or ovals. Cook for 3 to 5 minutes, or just until cooked through.
7. Add 2 cups (500 mL) scallop cooking liquid to soup. Add scallop balls to soup with green onions. Cook gently for 1 to 2 minutes. Serve sprinkled with coriander.

Maritime Chowder

In the Maritimes everyone has a different version of chowder. The only thing they agree on is that it shouldn't have tomatoes in it! I developed this recipe after a quick trip to Halifax with the Dini Petty Show. (If you do not want to use scallops or other shellfish, just use a little more fish.)

Serves 6 to 8

3 cups	water	750 mL	pinch	dried thyme	pinch
1 lb	haddock or halibut, cut into 2-inch (5 cm) chunks	500 g	1 cup	milk	250 mL
8 oz	fresh scallops, cleaned and cut in half if large	250 g	1 cup	light cream or milk	250 mL
			1/2 tsp	salt	2 mL
1 lb	potatoes, peeled and diced	500 g	1/4 tsp	freshly ground black pepper	1 mL
3 tbsp	unsalted butter	50 mL	2 tbsp	chopped fresh parsley, green onions or chives	25 mL
1	onion, chopped	1			

1. In large saucepan, bring water to a boil. Add haddock and cook for 2 to 3 minutes, or until barely cooked through. Remove fish to bowl.
2. Add scallops to liquid and cook for 1 to 2 minutes, or until barely cooked through. Reserve with haddock.
3. Add potatoes to liquid. Cook for 8 to 10 minutes until tender.
4. Meanwhile, heat butter in Dutch oven or large saucepan on medium-high heat. Add onion and cook for a few minutes until tender but not brown.
5. Puree half the potatoes with some of the cooking liquid. Add the puree and remaining potatoes and cooking liquid to the onions. Bring to a boil and add thyme. Add milk and cream and heat thoroughly. Cook gently for about 5 minutes.
6. Add fish and scallops and cook only until thoroughly heated. Add salt and pepper.
7. Serve with parsley, green onions or chives sprinkled on top.

A Lighter Side: Use half the amount of butter to cook the onions. Use milk instead of the light cream.

MISE EN PLACE   *This is a chef's term that refers to assembling all your ingredients before you begin to prepare any recipe. Cooking will be much easier and faster if you are organized. And be sure to read the recipe thoroughly before you begin.*

Peter Gzowski's Gazpacho

I love talking recipes with Peter Gzowski on CBC's Morningside. Peter doesn't like to measure ingredients or use a blender or one of those "things" (I think he means a food processor), but is a purist who adds things to taste and chops the ingredients coarsely with a knife. I sometimes like to add a little Tabasco sauce to this and serve it topped with homemade croutons sauteed in olive oil instead of the sour cream.

Serves 4 to 6

2	large ripe tomatoes, chopped	2
1	sweet green pepper, chopped	2
3	cloves garlic, minced	3
1/2 cup	extra-virgin olive oil	125 mL
	Chopped fresh chives to taste	
	Chopped fresh parsley to taste	
	Chopped fresh basil to taste	
3 tbsp	lemon juice	50 mL

1 1/4 cups	beef stock or classic brown stock *(page 99)*, cold	300 mL
1 1/4 cups	water	300 mL
1	large mild onion, thinly sliced	1
1 cup	diced, peeled and seeded cucumber	250 mL
1 1/2 tsp	salt	7 mL
	Freshly ground black pepper to taste	
1/2 cup	sour cream	125 mL

1. Combine tomatoes, pepper, garlic, olive oil, chives, parsley, basil and lemon juice in large bowl. Mix thoroughly.
2. Stir in beef stock and water. Add onions, cucumber, salt and pepper. Vegetables will float on top. Chill.
3. Serve with a spoonful of sour cream on each bowl.

Pappa al Pomodoro (Tomato and Bread Soup)

In Tuscany, they bake exquisite bread and don't like to waste it. That's how this recipe came to be. And in this day and age when our food costs are so high, this soup is a welcome inexpensive change. Be sure to use good-quality country-style bread that is a few days old. The texture is a bit odd — more like porridge than soup. But it definitely grows on you. Serve it hot in winter and cold or at room temperature in summer.

Serves 8 to 10

1/2 cup	extra-virgin olive oil	125 mL
3	cloves garlic, chopped	3
1/4 tsp	hot red chili flakes	1 mL
1 lb	country-style crusty bread, sliced and cut into chunks	500 g
4	fresh sage leaves, broken up (or 1/2 tsp /2 mL dried)	4
1	28-oz (796 mL) tin plum tomatoes, pureed with juices, or 1 1/2 lb (750 g) fresh tomatoes, peeled, seeded and pureed	1
5 cups	chicken stock or water	1.25 L
1 tsp	salt	5 mL
1/4 tsp	freshly ground black pepper	1 mL
1/4 cup	chopped fresh basil or parsley	50 mL

1. Heat oil in large saucepan or Dutch oven and add garlic and chili flakes. Cook for 30 to 60 seconds but do not brown.
2. Add bread and sage and turn to coat with oil.
3. Stir in tomatoes and stock. Liquid should just cover bread and tomatoes.
4. Add salt and pepper. Cook over low heat, stirring to prevent sticking, for about 15 minutes. Mixture will be thick. Taste and adjust seasoning if necessary. Stir in basil. Serve soup hot, at room temperature or chilled.

WINE SUBSTITUTES   *Try substituting lemon juice or a mild red wine vinegar for small quantities of wine in marinades, spreads, dressings, etc. But if a stew or cooked dish calls for a larger quantity of wine, use stock instead — chicken stock for white wine, and veal stock or beef stock for red wine. Instead of brandy, Cognac, Port or sherry, use some grated lemon peel, fresh herbs, Worcestershire or Tabasco — whichever seems most appropriate for the dish.*

6

Pastas

Fettuccine with Wild Mushroom Cream

This dish is very luscious and velvety, but it is rich, so I like to serve it only as an appetizer and in small portions.

Serves 8 to 10

2 oz	dried porcini mushrooms	60 g
1 cup	warm water	250 mL
3 tbsp	unsalted butter	50 mL
2	cloves garlic, finely chopped	2
1 lb	fresh button mushrooms, sliced	500 g
1 cup	whipping cream	250 mL
2 tbsp	Cognac, brandy or dry Marsala	25 mL
1 tsp	salt	5 mL
1/4 tsp	freshly ground black pepper	1 mL
1 lb	fettuccine (preferably fresh)	500 g
1 cup	freshly grated Parmesan cheese (preferably Parmigiano Reggiano)	250 mL
2 tbsp	chopped fresh parsley	25 mL

1. Place dried mushrooms in bowl and cover with warm water. Allow to soften for 20 minutes. Strain mushrooms through sieve lined with paper towel, reserving soaking liquid. Rinse mushrooms well and chop finely. Reserve.
2. Heat 3 tbsp (50 mL) butter in large skillet on medium heat. Add garlic. Cook gently for 1 minute until fragrant, but do not brown. Add fresh mushrooms. Cook for 5 to 8 minutes until any juices evaporate.
3. Add reserved wild mushroom liquid and chopped wild mushrooms. Cook for 5 to 10 minutes until liquid is almost totally absorbed by mushrooms and reduced. Add cream and cook until cream reduces and thickens. Add Cognac and bring sauce to the boil to allow alcohol to evaporate. Season with salt and pepper. Remove from heat.
4. Just before serving, bring large pot of water to a boil. Add 1 tsp (5 mL) salt and pasta. Cook until tender. Reheat sauce.
5. Drain pasta well. In large bowl, toss pasta with sauce, cheese and parsley. Taste and adjust seasoning if necessary. Sprinkle with freshly ground black pepper just before serving.

Spaghetti with Shrimp, Scallops and Red Peppers

Last year I was invited to Baffin Island to teach cooking at an International Women's Day event. It was a thrilling experience, even though I went in March and it was 75 degrees below on some days. (On a "warm" day, I was taken for an unforgettable early morning dog sled ride.) When I was trying to decide what to teach, I settled on Italian recipes using local ingredients. In this recipe I used the sweet scallops from Pangnirtung Bay and delicious baby Greenland shrimp. (If you use cooked shrimp, add them at the end when you are reheating the sauce.)

Serves 6 to 8

1/3 cup	extra-virgin olive oil	75 mL
3	cloves garlic, finely chopped	3
1/4 tsp	hot red chili flakes	1 mL
2	sweet red peppers, peeled, seeded and diced (optional)	2
12 oz	fresh scallops, cleaned and diced (or tiny bay scallops)	375 g
12 oz	shrimp, shelled, cleaned and diced	375 g
1 tsp	salt	5 mL
1/4 tsp	freshly ground black pepper	1 mL
1/4 cup	chopped fresh basil or parsley	50 mL
1 lb	spaghetti	500 g
1/2 cup	fresh breadcrumbs, toasted *(page 25)*	125 mL

1. Heat olive oil in large skillet on medium-high heat. Add garlic and chili flakes. Cook for a few minutes but do not brown.
2. Add diced sweet red peppers. Stir well. Cook for 5 to 8 minutes until tender.
3. Add scallops and shrimp. Cook for 2 to 3 minutes, or until seafood just turns opaque. Add salt, pepper and half the basil or parsley. Turn off heat.
4. Bring large pot of water to a boil. Add 1 tsp (5 mL) salt and spaghetti. Cook until *al dente* — cooked through but still firm to the bite. Drain well.
5. Turn heat on high to quickly reheat seafood sauce.
6. Toss spaghetti with sauce, breadcrumbs and remaining basil or parsley. Taste and adjust seasoning if necessary.

SCALLOPS   *I always try to buy fresh scallops, because their texture is usually far superior to the frozen. Before using the larger sea scallops in a recipe, you can clean them by pulling off the tiny piece of tough tendon on the side. This is where the scallop was attached to the shell. (This tendon is so small on the tiny bay scallops that this step isn't necessary.) If scallops appear sandy, rinse them.*

Linguine with Pesto Cream Sauce

This is a luscious combination of Genoa's famous pesto sauce with added cream to lighten the flavor and smooth the texture. The sauce would also be delicious served with the shrimp mousse (page 81) or Seafood Sausages (page 90).

Serves 8 to 10

3	cloves garlic, peeled	3
1/2 cup	pine nuts, toasted	125 mL
1/2 cup	packed fresh parsley leaves	125 mL
2 cups	packed fresh basil leaves	500 mL
3/4 cup	freshly grated Parmesan cheese (preferably Parmigiano Reggiano)	175 mL
1/2 tsp	salt	2 mL
1/2 tsp	freshly ground black pepper	2 mL
1/2 cup	extra-virgin olive oil	125 mL
3/4 cup	whipping cream	175 mL
1/4 cup	unsalted butter	50 mL
1 1/2 lb	linguine	750 g

1. Add garlic to blender or food processor and process until pureed. Add pine nuts and process until finely chopped.
2. Add parsley and basil and process until finely chopped. Blend in cheese, salt, pepper and oil.
3. In saucepan, heat cream and butter until warm. Stir pesto in just to warm through.
4. Bring large pot of water to a boil. Add 1 tsp (5 mL) salt and linguine. Cook until *al dente* — cooked through but still firm to the bite. Drain well.
5. To serve, in large bowl, toss drained pasta with warm pesto sauce. Taste and adjust seasonings if necessary.

A Lighter Side: Omit the whipping cream and butter and add 1/3 cup (75 mL) boiling water from the pasta to the pesto mixture to heat it up and thin it slightly. Toss with the pasta.

COOKING PASTA *Fresh pasta should be cooked until tender — about 1 minute for freshly made homemade pasta, or 5 to 8 minutes for the so-called "fresh" pasta from pasta shops. Dry pasta should be cooked for 8 to 12 minutes, until it is cooked through, but still firm to the bite. Always taste it to determine whether it is done.*

Spaghetti with Olive Paste

I tasted a dish similar to this at La Scala, one of Toronto's grandest Italian restaurants. Not only is this version delicious, it's really quick to prepare.

Serves 8

1/4 cup	extra-virgin olive oil	50 mL
3	cloves garlic, finely chopped	3
2	anchovies, minced	2
1/2 cup	black olive paste *(see below)*	125 mL
	Salt and freshly ground black pepper to taste	
1 lb	spaghetti	500 g
1/4 cup	chopped fresh parsley	50 mL

1. Place olive oil and garlic in skillet and cook gently on medium-high heat for a few minutes until very fragrant, but do not brown. Add anchovies and stir together well. Whisk in olive paste. Season with salt and pepper. Keep warm over very low heat or remove from heat and warm up just before serving.
2. Bring large pot of water to a boil. Add 1 tsp (5 mL) salt and spaghetti. Cook until *al dente* — cooked through but still firm to the bite.
3. Just before pasta is ready, stir about 1/4 cup (50 mL) hot water from pasta into the olive paste to thin it slightly and warm it.
4. Drain pasta and toss with sauce in large bowl. Adjust seasonings with salt and pepper. Sprinkle with parsley.

BLACK OLIVES *Unfortunately, it is almost impossible as yet to find really good black olives that have been pitted. The pitted olives that come in the tins are fairly sissy-tasting, so pitting the good ones is worth the effort. I usually use Kalamata olives when I need them pitted, because the tiny Niçoise ones (which are great on salads) are too small to pit easily. A good alternative to pitting olives, however, is to use olive paste, which is now available in many specialty food shops. Use two-thirds the amount of paste to whole pitted olives.*

Santa Fe Pasta with Shrimp and Chorizo

A spicy Italian sausage can be substituted for the chorizo. To cook the sausages, prick them and simmer for 30 minutes or barbecue for 20 to 25 minutes until cooked through. (Remove the casings from the sausages after cooking, if the casings are tough.)

Serves 8

3 tbsp	extra-virgin olive oil	50 mL
2	cloves garlic, finely chopped	2
1	4-oz (125 g) tin mild green chilies, chopped	1
1	jalapeño chili, finely chopped	1
2	tomatoes, peeled, seeded and diced	2
2	sweet red peppers, roasted, peeled, seeded and sliced	2
1 lb	chorizo sausage, cooked and sliced	500 g
3 tbsp	thinly sliced sun-dried tomatoes	50 mL
1 lb	shrimp, shelled and cleaned	500 g
1 lb	large macaroni pasta (rotini, penne, rigatoni or radiatore)	500 g
3 tbsp	unsalted butter	50 mL
1/3 cup	chopped fresh coriander	75 mL
	Salt and freshly ground black pepper to taste	

1. In large skillet, heat olive oil on medium-high heat. Cook garlic, green chilies and jalapeño for a few minutes until tender and fragrant.
2. Add fresh tomatoes, sweet red peppers and sausages. Cook gently for 10 minutes. Add sun-dried tomatoes and shrimp. Cook gently until shrimp are just cooked through, about 5 minutes.
3. Meanwhile, bring large pot of water to a boil. Add 1 tsp (5 mL) salt. Add pasta and cook until *al dente* — cooked through but still firm to the bite. Drain pasta well.
4. Stir butter and coriander into sauce. In large bowl, toss sauce with pasta. Taste and season with salt and pepper.

A Lighter Side: Use half the olive oil and half the butter. Use smoked chicken or turkey instead of the sausage.

Farfalle with Lobster, Asparagus and Lemon Cream

Farfalle is pasta in the shape of butterflies or bows. They are very delicate and whimsical, and this sauce suits them perfectly. Gentle and creamy, with the zingy flavor of lemon, this is perfect for the most sophisticated diner. Shrimp, scallops or smoked salmon can be used in place of the lobster. If you are using smoked salmon, simply dice it and add it at the end with the cooked asparagus. This dish is quite rich and expensive, so it is best served as an appetizer.

Serves 8 to 10

1 lb	asparagus	500 g		1 lb	cooked lobster meat	500 g
3 tbsp	unsalted butter	50 mL		3 tbsp	lemon juice	50 mL
1	clove garlic, finely chopped	1			Salt and freshly ground black pepper to taste	
pinch	hot red chili flakes	pinch		1 lb	farfalle or penne	500 g
1 cup	whipping cream	250 mL		2 tbsp	unsalted butter	25 mL
1 tsp	grated lemon peel	5 mL		2 tbsp	chopped fresh dill	25 mL

1. Wash asparagus and trim off tough ends. Peel stalks part way up with vegetable peeler. Bring water to boil in large skillet. Cook asparagus in boiling water just until tender and bright-green, about 5 minutes. Rinse with cold water to stop cooking. Pat dry. Slice on the diagonal into 1 1/2-inch (4 cm) pieces. Reserve.

2. Melt butter in large skillet on medium-high heat. Add garlic and chili flakes. Cook gently, without browning, for 1 to 2 minutes, until garlic is very tender and fragrant. Add cream and lemon peel. Bring to boil and reduce cream until slightly thickened, about 3 minutes.

3. Add lobster, asparagus, lemon juice, salt and pepper. Stir well and remove from heat.

4. Bring large pot of water to a boil. Add 1 tsp (5 mL) salt and pasta and cook until *al dente* — cooked through but still firm to the bite. Just before pasta is ready, reheat sauce.

5. Drain pasta well. Toss with sauce and butter in large bowl. Adjust seasoning with salt and pepper if necessary. Toss with dill.

CLEANING SQUID   *You can have squid cleaned by the fish store, or you can clean it yourself. First, separate the head from the body by running your finger around the inside of the sac. Remove the head and insides. Under cold water, peel off the thin skin and clean out anything inside the sac. You can open the sac and grill it like a fillet, or you can cut the sac into rings for fried calamari and salads. To clean the head, cut off the tentacles just in front of the eyes and twist out the hard bit of cartilage in the center. Discard everything except the round flower-like tentacle piece.*

Always cook squid quickly, or stew it for a long time.

Linguine Fisherman's Style in Packages

This is a newly revived way to serve pasta. When the pasta is baked in the paper, it absorbs any excess sauce and swells into puffy little bites. The texture is different, the taste is delicious, and the presentation is fabulous. You can even make the pasta ahead and reheat it in the packages. (If you prefer, serve the pasta without baking it in the paper. Just cook the linguine a little longer.)

Serves 8 to 10

3 tbsp	extra-virgin olive oil	50 mL
1	onion, chopped	1
3	cloves garlic, finely chopped	3
1/2 tsp	hot red chili flakes	2 mL
1	28-oz (796 mL) tin plum tomatoes, pureed with juices	1
1 lb	cleaned squid "fillets," cut into thin rings	500 g
8 oz	shrimp, shelled, cleaned and cut in half	250 g
8 oz	fresh scallops, cleaned and cut in half	250 g
	Salt and freshly ground black pepper to taste	
1 lb	linguine	500 g
3 tbsp	chopped fresh parsley	50 mL

1. Heat oil in large skillet on medium-high heat. Add onion, garlic and chili flakes. Cook for a few minutes until onion and garlic are tender and very fragrant. Add tomatoes, combine well and simmer gently for 15 to 20 minutes, or until thickened.
2. Add squid, shrimp and scallops. Cook for 2 to 3 minutes until seafood is just cooked. Season with salt and pepper.
3. Bring large pot of water to a boil. Add 1 tsp (5 mL) salt and linguine and cook until linguine is edible but still undercooked and slightly firm. Drain well and toss with sauce and parsley in large bowl.
4. Place 8 to 10 sheets of parchment paper or tin foil — approximately 12 x 18 inches (30 x 45 cm) — on the counter. Divide pasta among sheets. Spoon over any excess sauce. Fold over to encase pasta and secure edges with tiny folds as shown.
5. Place packages on baking sheets in a single layer and bake in a preheated 350°F (180°C) oven for 10 minutes.
6. Serve each guest one package on a large plate. Let guests cut packages open and eat pasta out of the packages. (Or you can just remove the pasta from the package and serve it on a plate or in a pasta bowl.)

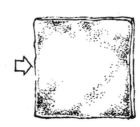

Pasta Norma

This Sicilian dish is named after the Bellini opera, "Norma." Bellini was from Sicily, and anything called Norma means the best.

Serves 8

1	large eggplant (1 1/2 lb/750 g) Salt	1
1/2 cup	extra-virgin olive oil (approx.)	125 mL
1	onion, chopped	1
2	cloves garlic, finely chopped	2
1/2 tsp	hot red chili flakes	2 mL
2	sweet red peppers, peeled, seeded and cut into strips	2
2	28-oz (796 mL) tins plum tomatoes, drained and pureed	2
	Salt and freshly ground black pepper to taste	
1 lb	penne	500 g
1/2 cup	freshly grated Romano or Parmesan cheese (preferably Parmigiano Reggiano)	125 mL
1/4 cup	chopped fresh basil	50 mL

1. Slice eggplant into rounds about 1/2 inch (1 cm) thick. Cut each slice into quarters. Place eggplant in colander and sprinkle with salt. Place in large bowl and allow to rest for 30 minutes. Rinse and pat dry.
2. Heat 1/2-inch (1 cm) olive oil in large skillet on medium-high heat. Cook eggplant in batches for 2 to 4 minutes per side, until golden. Drain well and reserve. Add more oil if necessary.
3. Heat 2 tbsp (25 mL) olive oil in skillet. Cook onions, garlic and chili flakes for a few minutes until tender and fragrant. Add sweet red peppers and cook for another 5 minutes. Add tomatoes and cook for 15 minutes. Season with salt and pepper. Add eggplant and cook for 5 minutes longer.
4. Meanwhile, bring large pot of water to a boil. Add 1 tsp (5 mL) salt and penne. Cook until *al dente* — cooked through but still firm to the bite. Drain well. Toss with sauce in large bowl. Top with cheese and basil.

A Lighter Side: Place the whole eggplant slices on a baking sheet and brush with oil. Broil until brown, turn, brush with oil and broil the second side. Cut the eggplant slices into quarters after broiling.

FRYING EGGPLANT   *To fry eggplant, in a deep skillet, heat at least 1/2-inch (1 cm) oil until very hot. Add the eggplant slices and cook until brown. Remove the slices from the skillet with tongs (not a spoon) and let the excess oil drip off. Drain the eggplant on a rack or paper towels.*

Spaghetti Puttanesca (Harlot's Style)

This pasta dish was one of the favorites of the ladies of the night in Rome. They said they could just whip it up between customers! I like it because it's so fast, you can just whip it up any time.

Serves 8

1/4 cup	extra-virgin olive oil	50 mL
4	cloves garlic, finely chopped	4
1/4 tsp	hot red chili flakes	1 mL
1 tbsp	anchovy paste (or 2 anchovies, minced)	15 mL
1	28-oz (796 mL) tin plum tomatoes, drained and chopped	1
1 cup	black olives (preferably Kalamata), pitted or unpitted	250 mL
1 lb	spaghetti	500 g
2 tbsp	chopped fresh parsley	25 mL

1. Heat oil in large skillet on medium-high heat. Add garlic and chili flakes. Cook for a few minutes until fragrant, but do not brown.
2. Stir in anchovy paste and tomatoes. Bring to a boil and cook for 10 minutes. Add olives. Cook for 5 minutes longer.
3. Meanwhile, bring large pot of water to a boil. Add 1 tsp (5 mL) salt. Add spaghetti and cook until *al dente* — cooked through but still firm to the bite.
4. Drain spaghetti well and toss with sauce and parsley in large bowl. Adjust seasoning with salt and pepper.

A Lighter Side: Use half the amount of olive oil.

Capellini with Lemon and Caviar

Good caviar is expensive. If I cannot afford sturgeon caviar in this dish, I use a more reasonably priced salmon caviar. It is very good for the price, colorful and delicious.

Serves 8 to 10

1 cup	whipping cream	250 mL
2 tbsp	vodka	25 mL
1 tsp	grated lemon peel	5 mL
1/2 tsp	salt	2 mL
1/4 tsp	freshly ground black pepper	1 mL
1 lb	capellini, linguine or fettuccine	500 g
1/3 cup	unsalted butter, diced	75 mL
2 tbsp	lemon juice	25 mL
2 oz	sturgeon or salmon caviar	60 g
2 tbsp	chopped fresh chives or green onions	25 mL

1. Place cream in large deep skillet and bring to a boil on medium-high heat. Add vodka, lemon peel, salt and pepper. Reduce heat and simmer gently for 5 minutes, or until sauce has reduced and thickened slightly. (This can be done ahead and the sauce reheated just before serving.)
2. Bring large pot of water to a boil. Add 1 tsp (5 mL) salt and pasta and cook until *al dente* — cooked through but still firm to the bite.
3. Place butter in large bowl. Add lemon juice to bowl.
4. When pasta is ready, drain well and place in bowl over butter. Pour sauce over pasta. Toss well until noodles are well coated with sauce and sauce thickens.
5. Serve pasta in individual pasta bowls or on plates and top each serving with a spoonful of caviar and a sprinkle of chives.

CAVIAR   *The most common sturgeon caviar are Beluga (large fish with big silver-gray eggs, and the most highly prized), osetra (medium-sized fish with smaller gray eggs) and sevruga (the smallest fish with darker, smaller eggs). I personally prefer the latter, and it's slightly less expensive to boot.*

I often use the less expensive but delicious salmon caviar (bright red with large eggs) in recipes as a garnish; golden whitefish caviar is also becoming popular. The common red or black lumpfish caviar is often so salty, I find it usually detracts from a dish rather than adding to it.

Spaghettini with Arugula and Radicchio

This is perfect for a summer appetizer or light summer dinner.

Serves 8 to 10

5	tomatoes, cored and diced	5
2	bunches arugula, coarsely chopped	2
1	head radicchio, coarsely chopped	1
2	cloves garlic, minced	2
1/4 tsp	hot red chili flakes	1 mL
1 tsp	salt	5 mL
1/2 tsp	freshly ground black pepper	2 mL
1/2 cup	extra-virgin olive oil	125 mL
1/2 cup	black olives (preferably Kalamata)	125 mL
1 lb	spaghettini	500 g

1. In large pasta dish, combine diced tomatoes with the arugula and radicchio. Blend in garlic, chili flakes, salt and pepper. Stir in olive oil and olives. Allow mixture to rest for 15 to 60 minutes so that flavors have a chance to mingle.
2. Just before serving, bring large pot of water to boil. Add 1 tsp (5 mL) salt and spaghettini. Cook until *al dente* — cooked through but still firm to the bite.
3. Drain pasta well and combine immediately with sauce. Toss until pasta is coated with sauce.

A Lighter Side: Use half the amount of olive oil

Penne Arrabiata

This is a very fast, easy pasta dish that is perfect for an appetizer. It tastes as if it is a lot of work to make, but it isn't. Because this appetizer is a little spicy, do not serve it before a mild main course.

This dish is not traditionally served with coriander or cheese, but I like to add them.

Serves 8

3 tbsp	extra-virgin olive oil	50 mL
4	cloves garlic, finely chopped	4
1/2 tsp	hot red chili flakes	2 mL
1	28-oz (796 mL) tin plum tomatoes, pureed with juices	1
1 tsp	salt	5 mL
1/2 tsp	freshly ground black pepper	2 mL
1/3 cup	chopped fresh basil or parsley	75 mL
1 lb	penne	500 g
3 tbsp	unsalted butter, diced	50 mL
2 tbsp	chopped fresh coriander	25 mL
1 cup	freshly grated Parmesan cheese (preferably Parmigiano Reggiano)	250 mL

1. Heat oil in large skillet over medium-high heat. Add garlic and chili flakes. Cook for a few minutes until fragrant, but do not brown.
2. Add pureed tomatoes, salt and pepper and cook for 15 minutes, or until sauce is medium-thick. Add half the basil. (The sauce can be made ahead to this point and reheated when the pasta is ready.)
3. Bring large pot of water to a boil and add about 1 tsp (5 mL) salt. Add penne and cook until pasta is *al dente* — cooked through but still firm to the bite.
4. Meanwhile, place butter in serving bowl. Drain pasta well and place in bowl with butter. Pour sauce over top, sprinkle with remaining basil and coriander and cheese. Toss well. Taste and adjust seasonings with salt, pepper and chili flakes.

A Lighter Side: Omit the butter and the cheese.

Penne with Four Cheeses

This creamy, luscious sauce gives the famous Alfredo sauce a run for its money. Serve this dish as an appetizer before a relatively light main course. And try fruit for dessert to help cut the wonderful but rich cheese and cream taste.

Serves 8 to 10

1/4 cup	unsalted butter	50 mL
2	cloves garlic, finely chopped	2
1 tsp	curry powder	5 mL
1 cup	whipping cream	250 mL
4 oz	Bel Paese or Camembert cheese, cubed	125 g
4 oz	Gorgonzola or other creamy blue cheese, crumbled	125 g
4 oz	fontina or Swiss cheese, cubed	125 g
1/2 tsp	freshly ground black pepper	2 mL
1/4 tsp	grated nutmeg	1 mL
1 lb	penne	500 g
1/4 cup	unsalted butter, diced	50 mL
1 cup	freshly grated Parmesan cheese (preferably Parmigiano Reggiano) Salt to taste	250 mL

1. Heat 1/4 cup (50 mL) butter in large skillet on medium-low heat. Add garlic and curry powder and cook very gently for 2 to 3 minutes, or until fragrant.
2. Add cream and bring to a boil. Cook gently for 5 minutes.
3. Add Bel Paese, Gorgonzola and fontina and allow to melt very slowly in the warm cream, about 3 to 5 minutes. Add pepper and nutmeg. (Do not worry if the cheese is not completely melted.)
4. Bring large pot of water to a boil. Add 1 tsp (5 mL) salt and pasta and cook until pasta is *al dente* — cooked through but still firm to the bite.
5. Place 1/4 cup (50 mL) diced butter in serving dish. Place dish over boiling pasta so that butter melts very gently and serving platter warms up.
6. When pasta is ready, drain well. Place in dish with butter. Add sauce, sprinkle with Parmesan cheese and toss well. Season to taste with salt if necessary. Serve immediately in warm pasta bowls.

Salad Risotto

When I took a group of cooking students to Giuliano Bugialli's classes in Florence, Italy, we cooked a lot, learned a lot, laughed a lot and ate so much we thought we'd burst! At one of the restaurants we visited we had a risotto that tasted like this. It is a lovely way to start a meal. Leftover risotto (if there ever is any) can be shaped into patties and sauteed in butter or olive oil for a sensational appetizer or lunch dish.

Serves 8

1/4 cup	unsalted butter	50 mL
1	onion, finely chopped	1
1	clove garlic, finely chopped	1
1 1/2 cups	short-grain Arborio rice	375 mL
1	small head Romaine lettuce, coarsely chopped (about 8 cups/2 L)	1
1 tsp	salt	5 mL
1/2 tsp	freshly ground black pepper	2 mL
5 cups	chicken stock, hot	1.25 L
3	green onions, chopped	3
2 tbsp	coarsely chopped Italian parsley	25 mL
1/2 cup	freshly grated Parmesan cheese (preferably Parmigiano Reggiano)	125 mL

1. Melt butter in a Dutch oven on medium-high heat. Add onions and garlic and simmer gently until tender and fragrant. Add rice and coat well with onion mixture.
2. Stir in lettuce and cook until wilted.
3. Add salt and pepper to stock. Add 1/2 cup (125 mL) hot chicken stock to rice. Stirring constantly, cook until liquid is absorbed. Continue to add stock 1/2 cup (125 mL) at a time, stirring constantly and cooking until each batch of liquid is absorbed before adding the next. It should take approximately 20 minutes to add the liquid, and the rice should be tender and creamy but still slightly *al dente* (you should be able to taste each grain of rice distinctly). Don't worry if you do not use all the liquid.
4. Stir in green onions and parsley and cook for 2 minutes longer. Stir in cheese. Serve immediately.

A Lighter Side: Use 1 tbsp (15 mL) butter to cook the onions and omit the cheese at the end.

Fettuccine with Chèvre

This was one of the most popular pasta recipes in the *CKFM Bonnie Stern Cookbook*. I like to serve it as an appetizer rather than as a main course because it is quite rich. Use a mild French or Canadian chèvre for a goat cheese tang that is not too overpowering.

Serves 8 to 10

1/4 cup	unsalted butter	50 mL
1	clove garlic, finely chopped	1
1 cup	whipping cream	250 mL
6 oz	chèvre (creamy mild goat cheese), crumbled	175 g
1 tsp	chopped fresh rosemary (or 1/4 tsp/1 mL dried)	5 mL
1 tsp	chopped fresh thyme (or 1/4 tsp/1 mL dried)	5 mL
1 tbsp	chopped fresh basil or parsley	15 mL
1 tsp	salt	5 mL
1/2 tsp	freshly ground black pepper	2 mL
1 lb	fettuccine	500 g
1/4 cup	freshly grated Parmesan cheese (preferably Parmigiano Reggiano)	50 mL

1. For sauce, melt 2 tbsp (25 mL) butter in large skillet over medium-high heat. Add garlic and cook for a few minutes without browning, until fragrant. Add cream and bring to a boil. Cook until liquid reduces and thickens slightly.
2. Whisk goat cheese into cream until smooth. Add herbs, salt and pepper.
3. Bring large pot of water to a boil. Add 1 tsp (5 mL) salt and fettuccine. Cook pasta until *al dente* — cooked through but still firm to the bite. Drain well. Toss in large bowl with sauce, Parmesan cheese and remaining 2 tbsp (25 mL) butter. Taste and adjust seasoning if necessary.

A Lighter Side: Use 1 cup (250 mL) pureed tomatoes instead of the cream. Cook for 10 minutes, then add the herbs, salt and pepper. Toss the cooked pasta with the tomato sauce and chèvre. Omit the Parmesan cheese and remaining 2 tbsp (25 mL) butter.

CHEVRE   *Chèvre is goat cheese. Although there is a huge range of goat cheeses available, when a recipe calls for "chèvre" it usually refers to a mild creamy version. Buy the rindless variety, or cut off the rind before using. There are some good domestic varieties, as well as the delicious but more expensive ones from France.*

Polenta with Wild Mushroom Ragout

I once did a presentation on food trends with chef Dominic Zoffranieri of the Delta Chelsea Inn. He was talking about how North Americans have discovered polenta, a dish he grew up with in Italy and learned to hate the way some children hate oatmeal. Zoffranieri said he came to Canada to escape from polenta, but it eventually followed him here! And now North Americans are learning to love it. This is a traditional Italian way to prepare it. For a creamier version, add 1/2 cup (125 mL) whipping cream to the polenta with the butter.

Serves 8 to 10

1 oz	dried porcini mushrooms	30 g
1 cup	warm water	250 mL
3 tbsp	extra-virgin olive oil	50 mL
3	shallots, chopped	3
3	cloves garlic, finely chopped	3
8 oz	fresh button mushrooms, sliced	250 g
8 oz	fresh wild mushrooms, trimmed and sliced (oyster, shiitake, cèpes, morels, chanterelles, etc.)	250 g
1 tsp	chopped fresh thyme (or pinch dried)	5 mL
1 tsp	chopped fresh rosemary (or pinch dried)	5 mL
	Salt and freshly ground black pepper to taste	
6 cups	water	1.5 L
1 tsp	salt	5 mL
1/2 tsp	freshly ground black pepper	2 mL
1 1/4 cups	yellow cornmeal	300 mL
3 tbsp	unsalted butter	50 mL
3 tbsp	chopped fresh parsley	50 mL
3 tbsp	chopped fresh basil	50 mL

1. In small bowl, soak dried mushrooms in warm water for 20 minutes. Strain liquid through a paper towel-lined strainer and reserve. Rinse mushrooms and chop.

2. Heat oil in large skillet over medium-high heat. Cook shallots and garlic for a few minutes until very fragrant, but do not brown. Add button mushrooms and soaking liquid from dried wild mushrooms. Cook for about 15 minutes until juices are absorbed by mushrooms. Add chopped dried mushrooms, fresh wild mushrooms, thyme and rosemary. Cook for 10 minutes longer. Season with salt and pepper. Reserve. (Dish can be made ahead to this point.)

3. In large saucepan, bring water to a boil and add 1 tsp (5 mL) salt and 1/2 tsp (2 mL) pepper. Whisk in cornmeal in a thin stream and cook over medium heat for 35 minutes, or until cornmeal starts to come away from pan. Stir almost constantly with a wooden spoon. Stir in butter, taste and adjust seasonings with salt and pepper.

4. Spread polenta out in a large shallow bowl or individual bowls. Pour hot mushroom mixture over top and sprinkle with parsley and basil.

7

Salads

Lentil Salad with Chèvre and Pine Nuts

Not only are lentil salads, soups and casseroles all the rage right now, they are healthy and really delicious. Serve this salad with cold cuts or as a terrific appetizer. I use the green lentils in salads, as they keep their shape better than the red when cooked. The salad can be made a day ahead, but do not place the lentils on the greens until just before serving.

Serves 8 to 10

1 1/2 cups	dried green lentils	375 mL		2 tbsp	chopped fresh chives or green onions	25 mL
4 cups	water	1 L		2 tbsp	chopped fresh basil	25 mL
1/4 cup	red wine vinegar	50 mL		1/4 cup	chopped fresh parsley	50 mL
2	cloves garlic, minced	2		6 oz	chèvre (creamy mild goat cheese) or feta, diced	175 g
1	shallot, minced	1				
1 tsp	Dijon mustard	5 mL				
1 tsp	salt	5 mL		1/3 cup	pine nuts, toasted	75 mL
1/2 tsp	freshly ground black pepper	2 mL		1	bunch arugula	1
3/4 cup	extra-virgin olive oil	175 mL				

1. Rinse lentils well and pick over, discarding any stones. Place in large pot, cover with water and bring to boil. Cook for 35 to 45 minutes, or until tender. Drain well.
2. For dressing, combine vinegar with garlic, shallot, mustard, salt and pepper. Whisk in oil.

3. In large bowl, combine dressing with warm lentils. Cool. Stir in herbs, chèvre and pine nuts.
4. Wash and dry arugula well. Trim away any coarse stems. Line salad bowl with greens and spoon lentils in center. Serve cold or at room temperature.

Salade Niçoise

This traditional southern French salad is making a big comeback these days with the focus on healthful provençal food and family-style French fare rather than haute cuisine. (In California, this salad is topped with thin slices of grilled rare fresh tuna instead of tinned.)

Serves 8 to 10

DRESSING

3 tbsp	red wine vinegar	50 mL
1	shallot or clove garlic, minced	1
1/2 tsp	dry mustard	2 mL
1 tsp	salt	5 mL
1/2 tsp	freshly ground black pepper	2 mL
3/4 cup	extra-virgin olive oil	175 mL

SALAD

1 lb	baby new potatoes	500 g
8 oz	green beans, trimmed	250 g
1	small bunch leaf lettuce	1
3	hard-cooked eggs, sliced	3
2	7-oz (196 g) tins tuna, or 1 lb (500 g) cooked fresh tuna	2
2	tomatoes, seeded and sliced	2
1/2 cup	black olives (preferably Kalamata)	125 mL
4	anchovies, chopped	4
2 tbsp	chopped fresh parsley	25 mL
2 tbsp	chopped fresh chives or green onions	25 mL
1 tbsp	chopped fresh tarragon (or 1/2 tsp/2 mL dried)	15 mL

1. For dressing, whisk vinegar with shallot, mustard, salt and pepper. Blend in oil. Reserve.
2. Cook potatoes in boiling salted water for 15 to 20 minutes, until tender. Drain well. Cut in half or slice, depending on size. Toss with 1/3 cup (75 mL) dressing and reserve.
3. Cook beans in boiling water, uncovered, for 3 minutes, or until barely tender. Chill quickly in ice water and pat dry. Toss with a few tablespoons of dressing.
4. Arrange lettuce on large platter or individual serving plates. Mound potatoes in center. Arrange beans and eggs around potatoes. Mound tuna on potatoes. Arrange tomatoes around outside edge of beans. Sprinkle with olives, anchovies and herbs. Drizzle remaining dressing over top.

A Lighter Side: Omit hard-cooked egg yolks and anchovies and use tuna packed in water or fresh tuna. When making the dressing, use 1/2 cup (125 mL) tomato juice in place of 1/2 cup (125 mL) of the olive oil.

Grilled Vegetable Salad

This is always a very exciting first course salad. You can vary the vegetables — just be sure to blanch the longer-cooking ones (such as broccoli and carrots) first so they do not burn on the grill. The croutons could also be spread with a chèvre quenelle mixture *(page 107)*.

Serves 6 to 8

3	zucchini	3
2	bulbs fennel	2
3	red onions	3
2	heads radicchio	2
12	oyster or shiitake mushrooms	12
	Extra-virgin olive oil	
6	slices French bread, 1/2 inch (1 cm) thick and about 3 inches (7.5 cm) wide	6
6	thick slices bacon	6

DRESSING

2	anchovies	2
1 tbsp	Dijon mustard	15 mL
1/4 tsp	freshly ground black pepper	1 mL
2	shallots, minced	2
1/4 cup	red wine vinegar	50 mL
1/2 cup	extra-virgin olive oil	125 mL
1/4 cup	chopped fresh basil or parsley	50 mL

1. Slice zucchini in half lengthwise. Cut tops off fennel and slice bulbs through the stems so that pieces stay together.
2. Peel onions and cut in half through the base. Cut radicchio in half. Trim stems off mushrooms if they are tough. Brush all vegetables with olive oil.
3. Heat barbecue or broiler and oil grill or broiler pan. Grill vegetables for 5 to 6 minutes, or just until tender. Turn frequently — use a wide spatula.
4. Brush slices of bread with olive oil. Grill bread until nicely toasted. Grill bacon slices. Drain on paper towels if necessary. Cut in half.
5. Cut vegetables as you wish and arrange attractively on individual salad plates. Top with bacon.
6. To make dressing, in bowl or food processor, mash anchovies and whisk in mustard, pepper, shallots and vinegar. Slowly whisk in oil. Season with salt only if necessary. Sprinkle dressing over vegetables and top with basil. Place a grilled crouton on each plate. Serve warm or at room temperature.

A Lighter Side: Grill vegetables without oil and omit bacon. Use half the dressing.

Tuna Carpaccio

Although this dish seems rather Italian, on my last trip to France I saw it on many menus. Be sure to explain to the person in the fish store that the fish must be absolutely fresh, as you are using it "raw." The salad can also be made with salmon or the more traditional beef fillet or sirloin — raw or cooked very rare.

Serves 6 to 8

1 lb	very fresh raw tuna or salmon fillet	500 g

MARINADE

1/4 cup	lemon juice or lime juice	50 mL
1/2 tsp	salt	2 mL
1/4 tsp	freshly ground black pepper	1 mL
1/2 cup	extra-virgin olive oil	125 mL
1/4 cup	chopped fresh coriander	50 mL
2 tbsp	chopped fresh chives	25 mL

DRESSING

2 tbsp	lemon juice or lime juice	25 mL
1/4 cup	walnut oil	50 mL
1/4 cup	extra-virgin olive oil	50 mL
	Salt and freshly ground black pepper to taste	
8 cups	mixed mild salad greens (mache, Boston lettuce, etc.)	2 L
2 tbsp	chopped fresh coriander	25 mL
2 tbsp	chopped fresh chives	25 mL

1. Wrap tuna or salmon and freeze for 45 minutes. Slice very thin and pound pieces gently with mallet until even thinner.
2. To make marinade, in bowl, combine lemon juice with salt and pepper. Whisk in oil and herbs. Spread some of marinade in large shallow dish and arrange slices of fish in single layer on top of dressing. Coat top of fish with remaining marinade. Allow to marinate in refrigerator for 20 minutes.
3. For dressing, combine lemon juice with walnut oil, olive oil, salt and pepper.
4. Just before serving, break greens into bite-sized pieces and toss with enough dressing just to coat. Arrange greens on individual plates. Top each salad with a few slices of fish. Sprinkle with coriander and chives. Serve immediately.

Bistro Salad

When I was in France last year, this was a common appetizer in many of the bistros and small restaurants I visited. And although I hadn't eaten chunks of bacon and visible eggs in a long time (watching cholesterol as we all are), I really enjoyed it. Even if you don't always make the salad with the bacon and eggs, you can use the dressing with a variety of greens.

Serves 6

8 cups	mixed salad greens, cleaned and dried well, broken into bite-sized pieces (arugula, curly endive or any bitter-edged greens)	2 L
8 oz	bacon, thickly sliced and cut into 1-inch (2.5 cm) pieces	250 g
6	slices French or Italian bread, cubed	6
2 tbsp	chopped fresh herbs (tarragon, parsley, coriander, chives, etc.)	25 mL
6	eggs (optional)	6

DRESSING

3 tbsp	red wine vinegar	50 mL
1	clove garlic, minced	1
1 tbsp	Dijon mustard	15 mL
1/2 tsp	salt	2 mL
1/4 tsp	freshly ground black pepper	1 mL
1/2 cup	extra-virgin olive oil	125 mL

1. Place greens in large salad bowl.
2. Place bacon in skillet on medium-high heat. Cook until crisp. Drain on paper towels. Discard all but a few tablespoons of bacon fat.
3. Add bread cubes to bacon fat and cook until crisp and brown. (If you are not using bacon, simply cook bread cubes in a few tablespoons of olive oil.) Remove bread and reserve.
4. Sprinkle greens with bacon, croutons and herbs.
5. To make dressing, in bowl, combine vinegar with garlic and mustard. Beat in salt and pepper. Whisk in oil gradually.
6. Poach eggs or pan-fry in a few tablespoons of unsalted butter.
7. Just before serving, toss salad with dressing and top with a freshly cooked egg.

A Lighter Side: Omit bacon and eggs. Do not fry croutons but bake them on a baking sheet in a preheated 400°F (200°C) oven for 5 to 10 minutes, or until browned. Use half the amount of dressing.

Caesar Salad with Pumpernickel Croutons

Instead of the usual croutons, the ones suggested here are made with pumpernickel bread and tossed with butter and cheese. They are even delicious just to nibble on!

Although many Caesar salads are overpowered with lots of anchovies and garlic, those flavors should really be more subtle.

Serves 6

1	large head Romaine lettuce	1

DRESSING

1	egg yolk	1
2	small cloves garlic, minced	2
3	anchovies, minced	3
1 tsp	Dijon mustard	5 mL
3 tbsp	red wine vinegar	50 mL
	Salt and freshly ground black pepper to taste	
1/4 tsp	Tabasco sauce	1 mL
1/2 tsp	Worcestershire sauce	2 mL
2/3 cup	extra-virgin olive oil	150 mL

1/3 cup	freshly grated Parmesan cheese (preferably Parmigiano Reggiano)	75 mL
2 tbsp	chopped fresh parsley	25 mL

CROUTONS

3 tbsp	unsalted butter	50 mL
3	slices pumpernickel bread	3
1/2 cup	freshly grated Parmesan cheese (preferably Parmigiano Reggiano)	125 mL
4	thick slices bacon, cooked until crisp and diced	4

1. Wash lettuce and dry well. Break into bite-sized pieces and place in large bowl.
2. To prepare dressing, place egg yolk in blender, food processor or bowl. Blend in garlic, anchovies, mustard, vinegar, salt, pepper, Tabasco and Worcestershire. Slowly dribble oil into mixture (use whisk if you are doing this by hand) until dressing begins to thicken. Add cheese and parsley.
3. For croutons, butter bread on both sides. Cut into 1/2-inch (1 cm) cubes.

Place on a baking sheet and bake in a preheated 400°F (200°C) oven for 5 to 10 minutes. Toss hot bread cubes in bowl with cheese until they are well coated. Cool.
4. Just before serving, toss dressing with lettuce. Garnish with croutons and bacon.

A Lighter Side: Omit bacon. Use only two-thirds the amount of dressing on the salad. Bake croutons brushed with 2 tbsp (25 mL) olive oil instead of butter and toss them with only 2 tbsp (25 mL) cheese.

Marinated Vegetable Salad

This is a colorful appetizer that is best served at room temperature. Only marinate this a few hours in advance, as some of the vegetables will lose their bright color if left to marinate too long.

Serves 6 to 8

1	small head cauliflower	1
1	small bunch broccoli	1
1 lb	asparagus or green beans	500 g
1 lb	carrots	500 g
2	tomatoes	2
1 cup	black olives (preferably Kalamata)	250 mL
1/4 cup	chopped fresh basil or parsley	50 mL

DRESSING

1/4 cup	balsamic vinegar or red wine vinegar	50 mL
1 tsp	salt	5 mL
1/4 tsp	freshly ground black pepper	1 mL
1	clove garlic, minced	1
1 tsp	dry mustard	5 mL
2/3 cup	extra-virgin olive oil	150 mL

1. Separate cauliflower and broccoli into florets. Trim tough base off asparagus and peel 1 inch (2.5 cm) up the stems. Trim beans if using. Peel carrots if necessary and cut into 2-inch (5 cm) sticks.
2. Steam or boil cauliflower, broccoli and carrots for 4 to 5 minutes, or until tender-crisp. Cook asparagus or beans for 2 to 3 minutes, until tender-crisp. Rinse vegetables with cold water to stop cooking. Pat dry.
3. Arrange vegetables in sections on large dish or individual plates. Slice tomatoes into wedges and arrange beside the other vegetables. Sprinkle with olives and chopped basil.
4. Prepare dressing by whisking vinegar in bowl with salt, pepper, garlic and mustard. Whisk in oil. Pour evenly over vegetables. Allow to marinate until ready to serve.

A Lighter Side: Use half the amount of olive oil in the dressing and add 1/3 cup (75 mL) chicken stock or sparkling mineral water. Use only a few olives as garnish.

VINEGARS *We used to think all vinegars were acidic and mean-tasting, but many that are available today are almost sweet. My personal favorites are a good-quality red wine vinegar, balsamic vinegar, sherry vinegar, raspberry and Champagne (white wine) vinegar. (And when you use a mild vinegar, you can add less oil to your dressings.)*

Balsamic vinegar has an almost cult-like following now in North America. It is a relatively new commercial product, although families in the area of Modena in northern Italy have been making it for themselves for centuries.

Specialty vinegars are usually unpasteurized, so after a few months they will form a kind of sludge in the bottom of the bottle. This is called a vinegar mother, which can be used as a starter if you want to make your own vinegar. Put the mother in a crock and add any leftover red or white wine to it. Leave it for a few weeks and, voilà, homemade vinegar. (Do not use pasteurized wine, or nothing will happen.)

Green Bean and Arugula Salad

Jean-Pierre Challet, the chef at The Inn at Manitou, gave me this recipe for my Quick Cuisine column in the Toronto *Star*. Sometimes people think French chefs can only cook long, complicated recipes. If you do, too, try this one.

Serves 4

8 oz	green beans, trimmed	250 g	1	shallot, minced	1
1	bunch arugula or other leafy lettuce	1	2 tbsp	chopped fresh chives Salt and freshly ground black pepper to taste	25 mL
1 tbsp	sherry vinegar	15 mL	1/3 cup	extra-virgin olive oil	75 mL
1 tbsp	lemon juice	15 mL			

1. Cut beans in half. Bring pot of water to the boil. Cook beans for 2 minutes until tender-crisp. Drain and chill under cold running water. Pat dry.
2. Wash lettuce. Pat dry. Tear into large pieces.
3. To prepare dressing, in large bowl, whisk together vinegar, lemon juice, shallots, chives and salt and pepper. Whisk in oil. Add beans to dressing and marinate for 15 minutes. Serve beans on a bed of greens.

SALAD GREENS   *There is such an array of salad greens available these days, I am surprised iceberg lettuce is still sold (although I hear it is about to make a comeback). For gently flavored salads, I love mild, buttery greens like Boston lettuce, mache, leaf lettuce or ruby-tipped lettuce. Tastes have changed so much that lettuces that were once considered bitter, such as Romaine and Belgian endive, are now considered sweet. Try using greens like curly endive (frisee), escarole, arugula and radicchio for a bitter edge.*

Wash greens well and dry them in a salad dryer or in tea towels. (If the greens are wet, the dressing will slip right off.) Break into bite-sized pieces or leave whole. To store greens in the refrigerator, wrap them in a tea towel and place in a plastic bag.

I usually count on about 1 1/2 cups (375 mL) greens per person. When adding the dressing, add a little at first and then toss well. Taste before adding more dressing (a salad that seems to need more dressing often just hasn't been thoroughly tossed).

Antipasta Salad

This is an unusual and pretty way to serve cold cuts. If you prefer, you can just serve the chickpea salad without the meats (make half the dressing).

Serves 8

8 oz	thinly sliced mortadella	250 g
8 oz	thinly sliced capocollo	250 g
8 oz	thinly sliced pepper salami	250 g
8 oz	thinly sliced provolone cheese	250 g
1	19-oz (540 mL) tin chickpeas, drained	1
1	6-oz (170 g) jar marinated artichokes, drained and chopped	1
1	sweet red pepper, roasted, peeled, seeded and diced	1
1/4 cup	black olives (preferably Kalamata)	50 mL
2 tbsp	chopped fresh basil or parsley	25 mL

DRESSING

1/4 cup	red wine vinegar	50 mL
2 tsp	Dijon mustard	10 mL
2	cloves garlic, minced	2
1/4 tsp	Tabasco sauce	1 mL
1/2 tsp	salt	2 mL
1/4 tsp	freshly ground black pepper	1 mL
3/4 cup	extra-virgin olive oil	175 mL

1. Cut the mortadella, capocollo, salami and cheese into very thin strips. Place in large bowl and toss together.
2. In another bowl, combine the chickpeas, artichokes, red pepper, olives and basil.
3. For dressing, in bowl, whisk vinegar with mustard, garlic, Tabasco, salt and pepper. Whisk in olive oil.
4. Combine half the dressing with the sliced meats and cheese and the other half with the chickpea mixture.
5. To serve, arrange sliced meats in a circle around the outside edge of serving platter or individual plates. Place vegetables in center. Serve at room temperature with crusty bread.

A Lighter Side: Use lean cold cuts such as roast turkey breast or roast beef. Omit the cheese and use half the dressing. Use canned artichokes instead of marinated ones.

Chicken Salad with Pesto

There are so many uses for pesto, and this is one of them. This dressing is also great on potato salad. Instead of the smoked chicken you can used smoked turkey or barbecued chicken, or you can smoke your own chicken in one of the new-style stove-top smokers that are now available.

If you make pesto in large batches for freezing, blanch the basil in boiling water for 5 to 10 seconds. Cool under cold water and pat dry. This will stop the basil from discoloring when frozen.

Serves 8 to 10

2 lb	boneless smoked chicken, cut into 1-inch (2.5 cm) chunks	1 kg
4	sweet red peppers, roasted, peeled, seeded and cut into 1-inch (2.5 cm) chunks	4
8 oz	bow-shaped pasta, cooked and drained and tossed with 2 tbsp (25 mL) olive oil	250 g

DRESSING

2	cloves garlic, minced	2
1/3 cup	pine nuts, toasted and chopped	75 mL
1/3 cup	freshly grated Parmesan cheese (preferably Parmigiano Reggiano)	75 mL

2 cups	packed fresh basil leaves, chopped	500 mL
1/2 cup	chopped fresh parsley	125 mL
1/4 cup	chopped fresh chives or green onions	50 mL
1/4 cup	balsamic vinegar	50 mL
3/4 cup	extra-virgin olive oil	175 mL
	Salt and freshly ground black pepper to taste	

GARNISH

4 cups	mixed salad greens, broken into bite-sized pieces	1 L
1 cup	cherry tomatoes	250 mL
1/2 cup	black olives (preferably Kalamata)	125 mL
	Sprigs of fresh basil	

1. In large bowl, combine chicken with red peppers and pasta.
2. For dressing, combine garlic, pine nuts, cheese, basil, parsley and chives. Whisk in vinegar and oil. Add salt and pepper.
3. Combine dressing with chicken. Stir gently but thoroughly to coat well.

Taste and adjust seasoning if necessary.
4. Serve on a bed of mixed greens. Garnish with tomatoes, olives and sprigs of fresh basil.

A Lighter Side: Use half the amount of oil, nuts and cheese in the dressing.

Corn Ensalada with Orange Chipotle Vinaigrette

When corn is not in season use frozen corn; this salad will still taste wonderful. The tortilla croutons are optional, or just use broken-up, good-quality corn chips.

Serves 6 to 8

4 cups	cooked or frozen corn niblets (about 8 ears)	1 L
1	sweet red pepper, roasted, peeled, seeded and diced	1
1	sweet yellow pepper, roasted, peeled, seeded and diced	1
1/4 cup	chopped sun-dried tomatoes	50 mL
4 oz	mild green chilies, diced	125 g
2 tbsp	chopped fresh chives or green onions	25 mL
2 tbsp	chopped fresh coriander	25 mL

DRESSING

1	small chipotle chili *(page 36)*	1
1	clove garlic	1
2 tbsp	red wine vinegar	25 mL
1 tbsp	frozen orange juice concentrate (undiluted)	15 mL
1/2 cup	extra-virgin olive oil Salt and freshly ground black pepper to taste	125 mL

TORTILLA CROUTONS

1/2 cup	corn oil	125 mL
4	corn tortillas Lettuce leaves (preferably Boston)	4

1. In large bowl, toss corn with red and yellow peppers, tomatoes, chilies, chives and coriander.
2. Puree all dressing ingredients together in food processor. Taste and adjust seasoning with salt and pepper. Combine with corn and marinate until ready to serve.
3. Meanwhile, heat oil in large skillet on medium-high heat. Cut tortillas into thin strips. Fry until crisp and drain on rack. Reserve. (If you have no time, simply break up good-quality lightly salted corn chips.)
4. Choose rounded lettuce leaves shaped like bowls and fill with salad. Top with croutons.

A Lighter Side: Omit the corn tortilla croutons. Use half regular orange juice and half oil in place of the total amount of oil in the dressing.

Grilled Eggplant, Red Pepper and Red Onion Salad

Grilled vegetables offer a wonderful smoky, outdoor taste. This salad is also a great accompaniment to main courses. The eggplants, red peppers and onions can also be broiled. You can make fabulous sandwiches in pita bread with this salad, and it is also a great pizza topping.

Serves 8 to 10

2	eggplants (1 lb/500 g each)	2
1 tbsp	salt	15 mL
	Extra-virgin olive oil	
2	red onions	2
3	sweet red peppers	3
1/4 cup	balsamic vinegar	50 mL
2	cloves garlic, minced	2
1/4 tsp	freshly ground black pepper	1 mL
1/2 cup	extra-virgin olive oil	125 mL
pinch	salt	pinch
1/3 cup	chopped fresh basil	75 mL

1. Slice eggplants into rounds approximately 1/4 inch (5 mm) thick. Place in colander, sprinkle with salt and allow to rest for 30 minutes. Drain off liquid and pat slices dry.
2. Heat barbecue or broiler. Oil grill or broiler pan. Brush slices of eggplant with oil and grill for approximately 3 or 4 minutes per side, or until brown.
3. Peel onions and slice into 1/2-inch (1 cm) rounds. Brush with oil and barbecue approximately 4 minutes per side, or until tender. Onions may fall apart as you turn them, but do not worry. Try to keep them whole but use rings if they don't stay together.
4. Grill red peppers until blackened on all sides, turning every couple of minutes. Remove from barbecue, cool, peel and cut into chunks.
5. Layer eggplant, onions and red peppers in large shallow salad bowl.
6. In small bowl, combine remaining ingredients except basil and pour over eggplant, red pepper and onions. Sprinkle with basil.
7. Allow to marinate until ready to serve. Serve at room temperature.

A Lighter Side: Use a very small amount of oil to brush over the vegetables while grilling. Use half the amount of oil in the dressing.

MESCLUM   *Mesclum is a mixture of about ten delicately flavored young greens. It is common in the area around Nice, and now this type of salad is offered in many fine restaurants in North America. Although there is officially an exact combination, you can use a mixture of any greens that are available, such as oak leaf, curly endive, arugula, escarole, chervil, dandelion and treviso.*

Mesclum Salad with Flowers

Even if some guests don't eat the flowers in this salad, they'll be talking about your dinner party for days!

Serves 8

1	head tender young radicchio	1
1	bunch tender young arugula	1
3	baby Belgian endives	3
1 cup	mache	250 mL
1/2 cup	edible flowers	125 mL

DRESSING

2 tbsp	Champagne vinegar or raspberry vinegar	25 mL
2 tbsp	orange juice	25 mL
	Salt and freshly ground black pepper to taste	
1/2 cup	extra-virgin olive oil	125 mL
2 tbsp	chopped fresh herbs (chives, basil, tarragon, parsley, coriander)	25 mL

1. Break up salad greens if necessary. Wash and dry carefully. You should have about 10 cups (2.5 L) loosely packed greens. Toss together with flowers in large bowl (break up petals where necessary).

2. Combine ingredients for dressing by whisking together vinegar with orange juice in small bowl. Stir in salt and pepper. Whisk in oil. Just before serving, sprinkle salad with dressing and herbs. Toss salad very gently.

EDIBLE FLOWERS   *Eating flowers is nothing new. It is just very much in fashion again. Flowers look lovely as a garnish on appetizer or dessert plates and are delicious when used in salads. Just be sure the ones you use are edible and pesticide-free. You can now buy packages of edible flower seeds, so you can grow your own to be on the safe side! Here are a few of the more common edible flowers: chive flowers, daisies, dandelion flowers, marigolds, nasturtiums, pansies, roses, impatiens, squash blossoms and violets. They all have very different tastes, so try them and see which ones you prefer. I usually use a very light-flavored dressing when flowers are in a salad — otherwise they will be overpowered.*

Mixed Seafood Salad

This is a very impressive appetizer salad. If you do not want to use shellfish, substitute about 3 lb (1.5 kg) firm-fleshed fish such as salmon, swordfish and/or halibut. You could also cook 1 lb (500 g) pasta and add it to this recipe. The pasta should be the commercial dry variety (about the same size as the pieces of seafood) such as farfalle or radiatore.

Serves 10 to 12

4 lb	mussels	2 kg
3 tbsp	extra-virgin olive oil	50 mL
3	cloves garlic, finely chopped	3
2 tsp	chopped fresh thyme (or 1/2 tsp/2 mL dried)	10 mL
2 tsp	chopped fresh tarragon (or 1/2 tsp/2 mL dried)	10 mL
1 cup	dry white wine	250 mL
1 cup	water	250 mL
1/2 tsp	freshly ground black pepper	2 mL
1 lb	squid, cleaned (page 124)	500 g
1 lb	shrimp, shelled and cleaned	500 g
1 lb	fresh scallops	500 g
8 oz	snow peas or sugar snaps	250 g
8 oz	carrots, cut into coins	250 g
2 cups	cherry tomatoes	500 mL
1	bulb fennel, cut into julienne	1
1/3 cup	black olives (preferably Kalamata)	75 mL
4 cups	mixed salad greens, broken into bite-sized pieces	1 L
3 tbsp	shredded fresh basil	50 mL

DRESSING

3 tbsp	lemon juice	50 mL
1	shallot, minced	1
1	clove garlic, minced	1
1 tbsp	Dijon mustard	15 mL
	Salt and freshly ground black pepper to taste	
3/4 cup	extra-virgin olive oil	175 mL

1. Clean mussels and remove beards. Discard any mussels with cracked shells, any that do not close when tapped and any that seem very heavy.
2. In Dutch oven, heat olive oil on medium-high heat. Cook garlic with thyme and tarragon for 1 minute. Do not brown. Add mussels, wine, water and pepper. Cover and steam until mussels open, about 5 minutes. Remove mussels from shells (saving the juices) and reserve. Discard shells and place all cooking liquid and juices in saucepan.
3. Meanwhile, cut squid into rings. (Use heads if you wish or discard.) Bring re-served cooking liquid to a boil and cook squid for 1 minute, or until just cooked. Remove and reserve with mussels.
4. Cook shrimp in boiling liquid for 5 minutes, or until cooked through. Remove and reserve with other seafood.
5. Remove and discard tough tendons from sides of scallops if you wish. Cook scallops in boiling liquid for 4 to 5 minutes, or until cooked through. Remove and reserve. Pour any accumulated liquid from bowl of seafood back into saucepan and reduce by half. Use 3 tbsp (50 mL) in dressing and freeze the remainder for soups or sauces.

6. Bring pot of water to the boil and cook snow peas for 30 seconds (cook sugar snaps for about 1 minute longer). Refresh in cold water, pat dry and cut in half on the diagonal. Cook carrots for 2 minutes, refresh and pat dry. In large bowl, combine snow peas with carrots, tomatoes, fennel, olives and seafood.

7. For dressing, combine lemon juice, reduced cooking liquid, shallot, garlic, mustard, salt and pepper. Whisk in olive oil. Taste and adjust seasoning.

8. Combine dressing with seafood mixture and allow to marinate until ready to serve. If serving within 30 minutes, do not refrigerate. Otherwise refrigerate until about 15 minutes before serving.

9. Just before serving, line salad bowl with greens, mound salad on top and sprinkle with basil.

Salad of Bitter Greens, Pancetta and Balsamic Vinegar

Bitter greens add a unique bite to a salad and urge your appetite forward into the meal ahead. Pancetta is unsmoked bacon that is available at Italian delicatessens and specialty stores.

Serves 8 to 10

1	bunch arugula	1	1/2 cup	pine nuts	125 mL
1	bunch chicory or escarole	1	1/4 cup	balsamic vinegar	50 mL
2	Belgian endives	2	2 tbsp	red wine vinegar	25 mL
1	small bunch fresh basil	1	3/4 cup	extra-virgin olive oil	175 mL
1 tbsp	vegetable oil	15 mL	1/2 tsp	salt	2 mL
8 oz	pancetta, sliced 1/8 inch (3 mm) thick	250 g	1/4 tsp	freshly ground black pepper	1 mL

1. Wash greens well. Tear into bite-sized pieces and dry thoroughly. Place in large serving bowl.

2. Brush large skillet with oil and heat on medium-high heat. Cook pancetta until crisp. Drain on paper towels. Cut or break into large pieces.

3. Return pan to heat and cook pine nuts in pancetta "oil" until lightly browned. Drain. Sprinkle salad greens with pancetta and nuts.

4. Discard remaining oil from pan and return pan to heat. Add vinegars and deglaze pan. Stir in oil. Add salt and pepper. Toss with salad just before serving.

A Lighter Side: Omit pancetta or use half the amount. Toast pine nuts on a baking sheet at 375°F (190°C) for 5 to 6 minutes instead of cooking them in oil. Use half the amount of dressing.

Mixed Salad with Parmigiano Reggiano

It is hard to believe that only twelve years ago in Toronto it was very hard to find Parmigiano Reggiano, one of the greatest cheeses in the world. It is so sweet and tender that you can eat it as a dessert cheese. And the price is comparable to inferior domestic varieties. In this recipe, I like to slice the cheese very thin rather than grating it.

Serves 6 to 8

8 cups	mixed salad greens	2 L	2 oz	Parmigiano Reggiano, sliced very thin	60 g
2 tbsp	red wine vinegar	25 mL	1/4 cup	sun-dried tomatoes, slivered	50 mL
1/2 cup	extra-virgin olive oil	125 mL	1/4 cup	black olives (preferably Kalamata), slivered	50 mL
1/2 tsp	salt	2 mL			
1/4 tsp	freshly ground black pepper	1 mL			

1. Wash and dry greens well. Break into bite-sized pieces. Place in salad bowl.
2. In small bowl, whisk together vinegar, olive oil, salt and pepper. Just before serving, toss lettuce with dressing.
3. Top with cheese, sun-dried tomatoes and olives. Toss well. Serve immediately.

PARMIGIANO REGGIANO *Parmigiano Reggiano is the original, best-quality Parmesan cheese. It is only slightly more expensive than the domestic version and one hundred times as good. You can buy it pregrated at cheese stores and Italian delicatessens, but it is better to buy a piece and grate it as you need it. Trim off the rind (which can be simmered in vegetable soups, etc.), and bring the cheese to room temperature before grating.*

Do not freeze Parmesan cheese. The pregrated cheese will keep for a few weeks in the refrigerator; larger pieces will keep much longer.

Warm Salmon Scallops with Lemon Vinaigrette

Although the salmon scallops are cooked at the last moment, this salad is very easy to prepare and everything else can be done ahead. Or you can serve the salad cold and do it all in advance. Slice the raw fillet on the diagonal into slices about 1/3 inch (8 mm) thick.

Serves 8

1 1/2 lb	very thin salmon scallops	750 g
1 tsp	grated lemon peel	5 mL
1/2 tsp	freshly ground black pepper	2 mL
8	large leaves ruby-tipped lettuce or Romaine	8
1 lb	asparagus or green beans	500 g

DRESSING

3 tbsp	lemon juice	50 mL
1	shallot, minced	1
1/4 tsp	Dijon mustard	1 mL
1 tsp	salt	5 mL
1/4 tsp	freshly ground black pepper	1 mL
1/2 cup	extra-virgin olive oil	125 mL
2 tbsp	chopped fresh dill or parsley	25 mL
2 tsp	chopped fresh chives or green onions	10 mL
8	cherry tomato roses (*page 4*)	8

1. Line baking sheet with waxed paper or parchment paper. Butter lightly. Arrange salmon scallops on sheet in one layer. Sprinkle with lemon peel and pepper. Cover with another sheet of buttered paper. Reserve until just before serving.
2. Rinse lettuce and pat dry. Arrange one leaf on each of eight salad plates (or do this just before serving).
3. Trim asparagus or beans. Cook in boiling water until just cooked and bright-green. Chill with cold water and pat dry. Arrange on lettuce.
4. For dressing, combine lemon juice with shallot, mustard, salt and pepper. Whisk in oil, dill and chives. Reserve.
5. Just before serving, bake salmon in a preheated 400°F (200°C) oven for 4 to 6 minutes, or just until fish barely flakes. Place one or two slices on each leaf of lettuce and spoon dressing over the top. Garnish each serving with a cherry tomato rose.

LEMONS AND LIMES   *Use fresh lemons and limes. Be sure to scrub them well before using the peel. You can freeze any excess grated peel, or freeze leftover juice in ice cube trays. To make a delicious Italian drink called a "canarina," place the peel of half a lemon in a mug and fill with boiling water. (Remove the peel in a continuous spiral for the most attractive presentation.) The water tastes wonderful and very different from hot water and lemon juice. The drink is a good digestive after dinner and perfect for early morning.*

Grilled Sirloin Steak Salad

If you love beef but want to cut back on the amounts you are eating, this is a perfect choice — small portions of rare, tender slices served on salad greens as an appetizer. You won't feel deprived.

Serves 8 to 10

2 lb	sirloin steak (about 1 1/2 inches/ 4 cm thick)	1 kg

MARINADE

1/3 cup	Dijon mustard	75 mL
1 tbsp	Worcestershire sauce	15 mL
1 tbsp	soy sauce	15 mL
1/2 tsp	Tabasco sauce	2 mL
1/2 tsp	freshly ground black pepper	2 mL

SALAD

10 cups	mixed salad greens	2.5 L
2	ripe tomatoes, sliced	2
1/4 cup	sherry vinegar or red wine vinegar	50 mL
1 tbsp	Dijon mustard	15 mL
1/2 tsp	salt	2 mL
1/2 tsp	freshly ground black pepper	2 mL
2/3 cup	extra-virgin olive oil	150 mL
1/2 cup	black olives (preferably Kalamata)	125 mL
2 tbsp	chopped fresh herbs (chives, parsley, basil)	25 mL

1. Trim excess fat from steak. Pat dry with paper towels.
2. Combine all ingredients for marinade. Coat steak with mustard mixture on both sides. Allow to marinate for 30 minutes at room temperature or overnight in refrigerator.
3. Heat barbecue or broiler and oil grill or broiler pan. Grill steak approximately 7 to 9 minutes per side for rare. If using a meat thermometer, the internal temperature should be 120°F to 130°F (50°C to 60°C). Allow steak to rest for 5 minutes before carving, or cool if serving salad at room temperature. Slice thinly on the diagonal.
4. Meanwhile, wash and dry greens thoroughly. Break into smaller pieces.

Arrange in bottom of large shallow serving dish. Arrange tomato slices around the edge.
5. Prepare dressing by whisking vinegar with mustard, salt and pepper. Beat in oil. Reserve. (Rewhisk just before serving.)
6. Arrange warm steak over greens. Sprinkle with olives. Drizzle dressing over top of meat. Sprinkle with fresh herbs.

A Lighter Side: Flank steak has a lower fat content than sirloin. If you use it instead, marinate it overnight in the marinade, to which you should add 1/4 cup (50 mL) red wine vinegar. Use half the dressing. (Or you could make this salad with grilled chicken breasts.)

Tabbouleh Salad with Feta Cheese

This is a perfect opening salad for a Middle Eastern dinner; it also goes very well with or before roast lamb or chicken. It can be served in hollowed-out tomatoes or mini pitas for an attractive presentation. You can use couscous instead of bulgur. Cook it according to the package directions.

Serves 6 to 8

1 cup	fine or medium bulgur	250 mL
	Boiling water	
1	English cucumber	1
1 tsp	salt	5 mL
2	tomatoes, diced	2
3	green onions, chopped	3
8 oz	feta cheese, drained and crumbled	250 g
1/2 cup	chopped fresh parsley	125 mL
1/3 cup	black olives (preferably Kalamata)	75 mL
3 tbsp	lemon juice	50 mL
1/3 cup	extra-virgin olive oil	75 mL
1/2 tsp	dried oregano	2 mL
1/4 tsp	freshly ground black pepper	1 mL
1	clove garlic, minced	1
	Salt to taste	

1. Place bulgur in large bowl and cover with boiling water. Allow to soak for 30 minutes. Place in strainer and press out any excess water, or wring out in a tea towel.
2. Meanwhile, peel and dice cucumber. Place in bowl and sprinkle with salt. Toss well. Allow to rest for 30 minutes. Discard accumulated liquid and pat cucumber dry.
3. In large bowl, combine bulgur with cucumber, tomatoes, green onions, feta cheese, parsley and olives.
4. Combine lemon juice, olive oil, oregano, pepper and garlic. Toss with salad. Taste and add salt only if necessary.

MARINADES *Marinades were once used to preserve foods, disguise the taste of foods that had already gone bad, and tenderize foods. We seldom use marinades for those purposes now. Although once in a while we may marinate a flank steak or round steak to tenderize it, our food is usually so tender to begin with that we generally use marinades for an extra boost of flavor.*

The longer food marinates, the more effect the marinade has. So if you are trying to tenderize something, marinate it overnight in the refrigerator.

Usually marinades contain an acid ingredient (lemon juice, wine, vinegar or yogurt), a little oil to keep the food moist and lots of flavorful ingredients such as mustards, herbs or spices.

Black Bean Salad with Corn and Red Peppers

I first served this on the Dini Petty Show. Jackie Vynen, one of the producers, liked it so much that she served it at her wedding. It was the first thing that disappeared!

Serves 10 to 12

1 1/2 cups	dried black turtle beans	375 mL
1 cup	long-grain rice (preferably basmati)	250 mL
1 tbsp	extra-virgin olive oil	15 mL
2 cups	cooked or frozen corn niblets (about 4 ears)	500 mL
2	sweet red peppers, roasted, peeled, seeded and diced	2
1/4 cup	chopped fresh coriander or mint	50 mL
1/4 cup	chopped fresh parsley	50 mL
6	green onions, chopped	6

DRESSING

1/4 cup	red wine vinegar	50 mL
2 tbsp	lemon juice	25 mL
1	clove garlic, minced	1
1 tbsp	chili powder	15 mL
1 tsp	salt	5 mL
1/4 tsp	freshly ground black pepper	1 mL
3/4 cup	extra-virgin olive oil	175 mL

1. Cover beans generously with water and soak for 3 hours or overnight. Drain. Place beans in large pot. Cover with plenty of water and bring to a boil. Turn heat to low and simmer very gently for 1 1/2 to 2 hours, or until beans are tender. Drain, rinse with cold water and drain well again.

2. While beans are cooking, prepare rice. Bring large pot of water to a boil. Add rice and cook, with water always at a boil, for 12 to 14 minutes, or until rice is tender. Drain in sieve. Toss with olive oil.

3. In large bowl, combine beans with rice, corn, red peppers, coriander, parsley and green onions.

4. For dressing, whisk red wine vinegar with lemon juice, garlic, chili powder, salt and pepper. Whisk in olive oil. Combine dressing with salad. Taste and adjust seasoning if necessary.

A Lighter Side: Use 1/2 cup (125 mL) orange juice instead of 1/2 cup (125 mL) of the olive oil. Use half the dressing on the salad.

Marinated Red Peppers

This is a great appetizer on its own, or you can use it as a topping on polenta, rice, pasta, salad greens, potatoes, pizza or bread.

Serves 6 to 8

8	sweet red peppers (or a mixture of red, green and yellow)	8
1/4 cup	capers (optional)	50 mL
1/2 tsp	salt	2 mL
1/4 tsp	freshly ground black pepper	1 mL
3	cloves garlic	3
2 tbsp	chopped fresh basil or parsley	25 mL
1/2 tsp	hot red chili flakes	2 mL
1/2 cup	extra-virgin olive oil	125 mL

1. Place peppers on baking sheet and broil until the skin blisters. Turn and blacken all sides. This may take 15 to 20 minutes (peppers can also be barbecued).
2. Place peppers in large bowl and cover with plate. Allow to cool and then peel them. Cut peppers in half, remove seeds and then cut into strips.
3. Layer pepper strips with capers, salt, pepper, garlic, basil and chili flakes. Pour olive oil over top.
4. Allow to marinate at room temperature until ready to serve, or refrigerate and then bring to room temperature before serving.

A Lighter Side: Drizzle only 1/4 cup (50 mL) oil over peppers.

OLIVE OIL   *Olive oil has become very popular lately, not only because it is delicious, but because it is a monounsaturated fat (now considered the most healthful, although generally it is agreed that we should cut back on all fat in our diet). Good olive oil has a full, fruity, sweet taste. Usually the best ones are called extra-virgin olive oils. These oils are cold pressed with no heat or chemicals used to extract the oil, and they have less than 1 percent acidity. But not all extra-virgin oils are equal, and many good oils are not extra-virgin, though it may require a bit of searching to find them.*

French olive oils are milder than others, with a light, flowery quality. Italian oils are more full-bodied and often spicy. Spanish oils are also becoming quite popular, and often they are a bit less expensive than the others and of very high quality. Generally, I use the best oil I have for salads, and less expensive oils for cooking.

Extra-virgin olive oil, once opened, keeps for about one month in a cool, dry, dark place. Refrigeration is not really recommended, but if you are not going to use the oil within a month, store it in the refrigerator. The oil may turn cloudy, but a few minutes at room temperature should bring it back to normal.

When I do not want the taste of olive oil, I use canola, safflower or corn oil.

Marinated Shrimp

I try to cook the shrimp in their shells to retain as much flavor as possible. If, however, you buy them already shelled, don't worry about it. Be sure to freeze the shrimp cooking liquid to use when a recipe calls for fish stock or shellfish stock. I like to use saltwater shrimp and prefer them fresh, but usually I can only find shrimp that have been frozen.

For an hors d'oeuvre, drain the shrimp and serve it on skewers or tooth-picks, or on rounds of bread.

Serves 6 to 8

4 cups	fish stock, chicken stock or water	1 L
1	onion, coarsely chopped	1
1	carrot, coarsely chopped	1
1	rib celery, coarsely chopped	1
2 tbsp	wine vinegar	25 mL
1 tsp	whole black peppercorns	5 mL
1 1/2 lb	shrimp in the shell	750 g
1/3 cup	lemon juice	75 mL
2/3 cup	extra-virgin olive oil	150 mL
1/4 tsp	freshly ground black pepper	1 mL
1/2 tsp	salt	2 mL
3 tbsp	chopped fresh basil or parsley	50 mL
4 cups	mixed salad greens, cleaned and dried	1 L

1. Place stock, vegetables, vinegar and peppercorns in saucepan and bring to a boil. Reduce heat and simmer for 10 minutes. Add shrimp still in the shell and cook just until they turn pink and curl, about 2 to 3 minutes.
2. Cool and remove the shells from the shrimp. Devein.
3. In large bowl, combine lemon juice, olive oil, pepper, salt and basil. Add shrimp and combine well. Allow to marinate until ready to serve. If serving within 30 minutes, do not refrigerate. If marinating for a longer period of time, refrigerate but allow shrimp to come to room temperature before serving. Place on bed of greens just before serving.

A Lighter Side: Use half the amount of olive oil.

Wild Mushroom Salad with Balsamic Vinaigrette

When the new organic market opened in Toronto, my husband, Ray, and I went to investigate. We bought the most delicious greens, and Ray came home and invented this salad. I should let him cook more often!

Serves 4 to 6

6 cups	mixed greens (arugula, Belgian endive, ruby-tipped lettuce, radicchio, etc.)	1.5 L
2 tbsp	unsalted butter	25 mL
2	shallots, finely chopped	2
2	cloves garlic, finely chopped	2
4 oz	fresh shiitake mushrooms, stems removed, sliced	125 g
4 oz	fresh oyster mushrooms, stems removed, sliced	125 g
4 oz	fresh button mushrooms, sliced	125 g
1/2 tsp	salt	2 mL
1/2 tsp	freshly ground black pepper	2 mL
2 tbsp	chopped fresh chives or green onions	25 mL
2 tbsp	chopped fresh parsley	25 mL
3 tbsp	balsamic vinegar	50 mL
1/3 cup	extra-virgin olive oil	75 mL

1. Dry greens well, break into bite-sized pieces and place in salad bowl.
2. Heat butter in large skillet on medium-high heat. Add shallots and garlic. Cook until fragrant.
3. Add mushrooms and cook for 5 to 8 minutes, until mushrooms are wilted and tender. Season with salt, pepper, chives and parsley. Spoon over salad.
4. Add vinegar and oil to skillet and heat gently just until warm. Pour over salad and toss gently.

SHALLOTS   *Shallots are actually a member of the lily family. They almost taste like a combination of onions and garlic. If you are using them raw, soak them for 10 minutes in ice water and then wring them dry in a tea towel. This softens the taste.*

If you do not have shallots, there are a number of substitutes. In a salad, I usually substitute green onions. In cooked dishes, I usually use half an onion and half a clove of garlic for each shallot.

Pacific Rim Swordfish Salad

When Hugh Carpenter came to teach at the school, he inspired us all to experiment with Asian ingredients. This was one East-meets-West result.

Serves 6

DRESSING

2 tbsp	lemon juice	25 mL
1/4 cup	extra-virgin olive oil	50 mL
1/2 tsp	oriental chili paste	2 mL
2 tbsp	soy sauce	25 mL
1 tbsp	honey	15 mL
1 tsp	oriental sesame oil	5 mL

MARINADE

1 tbsp	hoisin sauce	15 mL
1 tbsp	soy sauce	15 mL
1 tbsp	rice wine or mirin	15 mL

1	clove garlic, minced	1
1 tsp	chopped fresh ginger root	5 mL
1 lb	swordfish, sliced 1/4 inch (5 mm) thick	500 g
2 tbsp	extra-virgin olive oil	25 mL
8 cups	mixed salad greens, broken into bite-sized pieces	2 L
1/4 cup	chopped fresh coriander	50 mL
1/4 cup	chopped fresh chives or green onions	50 mL

1. To make dressing, in large bowl, whisk lemon juice with oil, chili paste, soy sauce, honey and sesame oil. Reserve.
2. To make marinade, in bowl, combine hoisin sauce, soy sauce, rice wine, garlic and ginger.
3. Pat fish dry and cut into 2-inch (5 cm) pieces. Combine with marinade, toss and marinate for about 10 minutes.
4. Just before serving, heat 2 tbsp (25 mL) olive oil in large skillet or wok. Add fish and toss well, cooking until barely cooked through. Add dressing and combine gently.
5. Place greens in wide shallow bowl. Pour dressing and fish over salad greens.
6. Sprinkle with fresh coriander and chives and toss.

SPECIALTY OILS *Walnut oils and other nut oils are used for flavor, but not in great quantity. Keep them refrigerated and use them as quickly as possible, as they go rancid easily.*

Oriental sesame oil is usually used as a last-minute flavoring to add a strong taste of toasted sesame seed. Store it in the refrigerator.

Index